EXTERNAL REPORTING FOR SEGMENTS OF A BUSINESS

By

Morton Backer, Ph.D., CPA,

Professor of Accounting, University of Massachusetts

and

Walter B. McFarland, Ph.D.,

Research Director, National Association of Accountants

DIGEST OF FINDINGS FROM
NAA RESEARCH STUDY

O PERATING RESULTS for segments of diversified companies can be reported in ways which meet needs expressed by investors. The fact that this can be done with a comparatively few broad segments tends to minimize possible harmful reactions from disclosure. Reporting of sales and contributions to consolidated profits by significant segments can be accomplished by adapting accounting techniques now used by some companies for internal management purposes.

To cut through the existing uncertainty about what information is needed, depth interviews with financial analysts and bankers were first employed to identify the specific kinds of segment financial data relevant to investors' and creditors' decision-making processes. Both groups were found to be primarily interested in data serviceable for estimating future earnings. In evaluating investment or credit strength of a diversified company, separate forecasts are made for each industry or market in which the company has a material participation. Income is projected for each segment and combined for conversion to earnings per share for the company under analysis.

The report states that management in each company can best define the segments for which to report provided it meets the needs which suppliers of capital have for information. Usefulness in forecasting requires that each segment be relatively homogeneous in its response to economic conditions. Significant segments are usually groups of end-products, but markets are sometimes primary or supplementary segments for reporting. While they simulate forecasting procedures which companies employ for internal information, outsiders need information only for segments having a material effect on consolidated earnings. No standard classification of segments for reporting can yield meaningful results when applied to companies with diverse organizational patterns. Uniformity for all companies is not essential because skilled analysts do not regard intercompany comparisons of segment results to be significant in their work.

Presence of both joint revenues and joint costs makes it impossible to determine net profit for individual segments except with arbitrary allocations which tend to destroy validity of the resulting figures as measures of individual segment contributions to overall profits. Where segments are linked together by a limited number of common functions, contribution margins are reliable and useful for forecasting segment contributions to common costs and aggregate profits. Segment contribution margin is the excess of separable revenues over separable costs of a segment. Where operations are highly integrated and separable contributions by segments are small relative to the amount of joint cost, segments in the combination are best treated as a single unit for external reporting.

Disclosure of sufficient detail to enable users of segment reports to distinguish short-run variable, annual programmed, and long-run capacity costs will be helpful in forecasting earnings.

In a final phase of the study, executives of 70 large companies were interviewed to ascertain their reactions to conclusions drawn from the preceding phases. No serious opposition to segment sales was found but, with some exceptions, opposition to disclosure of segment contributions to profits was strong. Major reasons given for attitudes expressed were (1) that earnings figures meaningful to outsiders cannot be constructed for anything less than the whole enterprise and (2) fear that disclosure of segment earnings margins may provoke reactions from outsiders detrimental to welfare of the stockholders. However, the study suggests that reporting techniques can be developed to provide useful segment earnings and that some company executives probably underrate analysts' sophistication and skills. The fact that outsiders' information needs can be met with a comparatively few broad segments tends to minimize harmful reactions from disclosure.

The foregoing conclusions are supported by experience of a few companies that now report segment earnings. Executives of these companies stated that the practice has improved understanding of their companies in the financial community with no objectional reactions of consequence.

The report suggests that investors' confidence in reports on segment operations will be improved if independent auditors can accept responsibility for segment data by expressing an opinion on financial statements available to stockholders and creditors.

Research Study published by

National Association of Accountants

505 Park Avenue, New York, N. Y. 10022

EXTERNAL REPORTING
FOR
SEGMENTS OF A BUSINESS

By

Morton Backer, Ph.D., CPA,

Professor of Accounting, University of Massachusetts

and

Walter B. McFarland, Ph.D.,

Research Director, National Association of Accountants

List Price $2.50

Research Study published by

National Association of Accountants

505 Park Avenue, New York, N. Y. 10022

Copyright by the National Association of Accountants © April 1968

CONTENTS

Chapter 1. Uses for Reports on Segment Operations........ 1

Chapter 2. Technical Problems in Segment Reporting...... 15

Chapter 3. Contribution Margin Reporting................ 28

Chapter 4. Current Disclosure Practices 41

Chapter 5. External Reporting for Legal Corporate Segments 65

Chapter 6. Reactions of Corporate Executives to Segment Reporting 77

Chapter 7. Conclusions 99

NAA Research Studies in Management Reporting

This is the first in the NAA Research Series in Management Reporting, which will comprise studies dealing with management's discharge of its responsibilities for reporting economic information to external groups including stockholders, creditors, and government.

iv

REPORT REVIEW COMMITTEE

NAA ORGANIZATION FOR RESEARCH

NAA research reports are presented in furtherance of the Association's educational objectives in the field of managerial accounting. These objectives are (1) to provide leadership in the continuing evolutionary development of managerial accounting, (2) to disseminate knowledge of managerial accounting techniques and their uses, and (3) to encourage wider adoption of the best practices.

Research projects are initiated by the Research Planning Committee, acting with approval of the National Board of Directors. The Research Staff collects information, analyzes this material, and prepares reports presenting findings. When it is the consensus of the Committee that a research report merits consideration, publication is recommended. Contents of reports present findings and conclusions drawn by those who did the research and do not necessarily reflect views of research committee members.

CHAPTER 1

Uses for Reports on Segment Operations

SUMMARY

This report presents findings and conclusions on external reporting for segments of diversified companies from an NAA research project titled *Financial Reporting for Investment and Credit Decisions*. In view of current interest in the topic, these findings have been made available before publication of the results from the broader study.

Major questions considered in this report are (1) defining segments which are significant to suppliers of capital and (2) what kinds of segment financial information can best serve these users' purposes. The study adopts the hypothesis that financial information relevant to investors' and creditors' needs can be identified by studying how these groups make decisions. Depth interviews with carefully chosen groups of financial analysts and commercial bankers were employed to learn what these skilled users of financial reports look for and what their attitudes are toward such reports. In a subsequent series of interviews, reactions were obtained from executives of 70 large companies.

Individual segments of diversified companies are af-

1

fected differently by economic conditions and have different rates of growth, risk, and profitability. Hence analysis underlying appraisals of investment or credit worth for such a company require measures of segment contributions to enterprise revenues and profits. Objectives of this analysis are to ascertain relative size of the various components, to build up forecasts of consolidated income by major segments, and to gain insight into success of diversification actions. Segment financial data are not wanted for intercompany comparisons at the segment level since analysts interviewed are aware that such comparisons would rarely be meaningful.

Business executives interviewed expressed opinion to the effect that fuller disclosure of segment sales and income will be required in the future and most agreed that such information is needed by investors and creditors.

PUBLIC REPORTING OF operating results for segments of diversified businesses has been widely discussed during the past three years. Strong impetus was given to such discussion by a series of hearings before the Senate Subcommittee on Antitrust and Monopoly together with various public remarks by Manuel Cohen, Chairman of the Securities and Exchange Commission.[1] However, it is unlikely that these Senate hearings would have provoked so much attention had there not been widespread opinion in the financial community to the effect that more disclosure of segment operating results is needed.

The SEC appears to possess the requisite authority, under existing law, to require disclosure of such information and its regulations call for a limited amount of segment financial data in registration statements filed with the Commission.[2] The likelihood that such requirements may be broadened and effectively enforced has raised numerous questions with regard to how meaningful and useful public segment reports can be prepared. It has also led to contro-

---

[1] See "The SEC and Accountants: Co-operative Efforts to Improve Financial Reporting," *Journal of Accountancy*, December 1966, pp. 56-60.

[2] Hearings before the Subcommittee on Antitrust and Monopoly, Committee on the Judiciary, United States Senate, Eighty-Ninth Congress, First Session, pp. 1069-71; A. A. Sommer, Jr., "Conglomerate Disclosure: Friend or Foe," *Journal of Accountancy*, May 1967.

versy over how much segment information can be disclosed without serious damage to stockholders, creditors, and others.

In response to these questions, the Accounting Principles Board stated that:[3]

> "The Board recognizes that such information may be useful for investors in appraising past performance and future risks and prospects of diversified companies."

The Financial Executives Institute initiated a research study focused on problems which arise in reporting for segments of a business. A study started by NAA late in 1964 also throws significant light on the subject, although this was not among the original objectives of the study. This study, titled *Financial Reporting for Security Investment and Credit Decisions*, was designed to test the hypothesis that the kinds of financial information relevant to investor's and creditor's purpose can be ascertained by studying how these groups make decisions and that such knowledge can be a useful guide to financial reporting practice.[4]

Sources of Information

To determine how financial information is used in making equity investment decisions, 72 carefully selected financial analysts were interviewed. Helpful assistance in selecting these individuals was received from the New York Society of Security Analysts. Since recommendations made by members of the group interviewed influence actions of both large institutional investors and many individual investors, it seems reasonable to expect that the interviewees are representative of skilled professional users of financial reports in investment decision-making. In a similar fashion, 71 commercial bankers (about half of whom were senior loan officers and half were senior credit analysts) were interviewed to learn how financial information is used in making short- and long-term credit decisions. The Robert Morris Associates and the American Bankers Association provided guidance in chosing bankers who were asked to participate in the study.

In each instance, interviewees were asked to describe any im-

---

[3] *Disclosure of Supplement Financial Information by Diversified Companies*, September 1967.

[4] This approach to research was pioneered by NAA in its studies of accounting to serve internal management purposes. A strong suggestion that accounting research should look to the needs of individual users as a guide to the development of accounting theory and methods is also contained in *A Statement of Basic Accounting Theory*, issued by the American Accounting Association in 1966. This approach has not yet been extensively applied in external financial reporting. Instead, most research has sought to derive principles from subjective postulates such as fairness, rationality, and nondistortion or to prescribe individual accounting procedures because they are found to be generally accepted.

portant shortcomings they found in the financial reports they use.[5] Absence of information about operating results for major segments of diversified companies was mentioned in almost every interview. That the topic deserves high priority in attempts to improve the usefulness of financial reports was the virtually unanimous opinion of analysts and bankers participating in the study. This finding was not anticipated when the study was planned.

In a subsequent phase of the study, executives of 70 large industrial corporations were interviewed to ascertain the reasons underlying their companies' financial reporting practices and to learn their reactions to findings from discussions with the two financial statement user groups. Corporate executives interviewed were, in each company, active participants in establishing their company's external reporting policies. Here also reporting segment results was a topic possessing very high current interest.

This report summarizes findings from that portion of the study concerned with external reporting for segments of a business. Utilizing both empirical research and analysis, certain conclusions are drawn as to what kind of segment reports will be useful and suggestions are offered for putting conclusions into practice.

Demand for Segment Reports

Viewed in perspective, the current demand for public reporting of segment operating results appears as the product of several converging trends. The one deserving mention first is the growth, both in absolute size and in depth, of the market for industrial capital in the United States. Prominent in this growth has been emergence of large institutional investors such as pension funds and mutual funds. At the same time, older financial institutions such as commercial banks and insurance companies have become major suppliers of long-term capital. Individual investors have also become more numerous and more knowledgeable. Both institutional and individual investors are served by professional investment analysts and managers whose technical skills and sophistication have advanced rapidly.

Continuing needs for capital and awareness of the latent power possessed by shareholders and creditors have made business managers increasingly conscious of company image in the eyes of the financial community. Discussions with all three groups of inter-

---

[5] Specific questions were also asked regarding topics such as inventory costing, accounting for depreciation, research and development, goodwill, and price level changes. Findings from the entire study will be presented in an NAA research publication now in preparation.

viewees in this study lent considerable credence to the belief that frank disclosure of information, both favorable and unfavorable, tends to improve a company's image among investors and creditors. That adequate and reliable financial information is a matter of public interest has also been recognized by the Federal Government and since the nineteen thirties, the SEC has exerted a potent influence on financial reporting practices.

Influence of Business Diversification

The general demand for more and better financial information by investors, creditors, and those who serve them has recently been focused upon segments of diversified businesses. Strong pressure to convert discussion into action has been created by public expressions of concern on the part of the SEC. All of the foregoing factors in combination have led some companies to institute disclosure of segment results in varying degrees and ways.[6] The same influences have caused nearly all of the companies participating in this study to give serious consideration to possible future disclosure.

The controversy over reporting segment operating results has its setting in the widespread movement toward diversification in enterprises, both large and small. While diversification is not new, the trend has accelerated in recent years until diversification is not usual rather than exceptional among companies large enough to seek public financing. The aspect most significant for financial reporting has been the markedly increased number of so-called "conglomerate" enterprises. Thus, in reporting on one phase of a study by the Financial Executives Institute, Robert K. Mautz has stated that:[7]

> ". . . a conglomerate company is defined as one which is so managerially decentralized, so lacks operational integration, or has such diversified markets that it may experience rates of profitability, degrees of risk, and opportunities for growth which vary within the company

[6] "A comparative survey of the 1965 and 1966 annual reports of 241 large companies (sales over $100 million) showed that the number of companies providing a breakdown of sales on a segmented basis increased from 37% to 51% of the total. Oddly, there were some backsliders—seven companies had furnished such breakdowns in 1965 but not in 1966. In an expanded group of 331 companies, we noted 24 which gave substantial disclosure on the profit contributions of their different product lines or divisions . . . while this figure is not large, it should be kept in mind that very few companies provided such disclosures in 1965 and that many of the companies surveyed were not widely diversified.

"In a recent survey of 265 filings (prospectuses) under the 1933 Act by companies with sales in excess of $25 million, we found that 9.7% of the companies provided breakdowns on net income or relative contributions to net profit. We believe these data may also be indicative of further improvements in subsequent annual reports." (Andrew Barr, "Comments on the Conglomerate Reporting Problem," *Financial Executive*, November 1967, p. 45.)

[7] "Identification of the Conglomerate Company," *Financial Executive*, July 1967, p. 26

to such an extent that an investor requires information about these variations in order to make informed decisions."

Terminology Employed in this Study

Since diversification is the general condition which has led to a demand for external reporting of operating results for subdivisions of companies, this study considers the possible usefulness and the technical aspects of preparing such reports for a broad range of diversified companies. The study is not restricted to the conglomerate type of diversification because, to meet the needs expressed by security analysts, reporting of segment financial data must extend to many companies which are not conglomerates. In fact, a majority of the companies whose securities are publicly traded probably fall in this class. When bank loan officers' information needs are considered, even many small businesses have products or markets which need to be analyzed separately. The effects which different company organization patterns have on segment reporting are discussed in Chapter 2.

The fact that financial reporting practices have already advanced so far in the United States provides an environment in which suppliers of capital recognize the need for and have the competence to use segment reports. At the same time, developments in the underlying accounting systems to guide applications of company resources make it possible to produce meaningful segment reports. In many other countries, management seldom has reliable measures of segment contribution to enterprise profit and investors often do not even receive consolidated sales.[8]

EXPRESSED NEEDS FOR SEGMENT
OPERATING RESULTS

Expressions of need for information about the component segments of individual businesses have come from three principal groups of users of corporate financial reports. These are, in the order discussed below, (1) financial analysts and underwriters concerned principally with equity securities, (2) commercial bankers who extend both short- and long-term business credit, and (3) various governmental agencies. For purposes of the study, these groups have been drawn upon as sources of information about how segment operating results are, or might be, used for making investment decisions, for making credit decisions, and for preparing and administering laws. The last is considered only briefly with information being drawn from secondary sources.

---

[8] However, it may be noted that the British Companies Act of 1967 requires disclosures of sales and profits for certain segments of businesses.

6

Uses in Making Security Investment Decisions

Over the past half century, the nature of equity investments has drastically changed. In most large companies, the dual function exercised by the individual owner-manager has been separated. Operations has become the responsibility of professional managers while equity capital is drawn primarily from a large group of investors divorced from managerial authority. Shareholders often change rapidly as they seek to take advantage of shifting opportunities. Isolated from management's detailed knowledge, investors are compelled to rely upon information disclosed by companies together with collateral information from various outside sources. Collection, analysis and interpretation of such information has become a specialized function performed by expert security analysts. Both rational individual investors and managers of investment funds now rely heavily on advice from professional analysts who have competence, access, and time to study information not ordinarily possessed by those who make investment decisions.

In the course of the broad NAA study previously described, financial analysts were asked a series of specific questions designed to bring out the manner in which they use information ordinarily presented in consolidated financial statements. At the conclusion of this portion of each interview, the interviewees were asked to list and to comment on any significant shortcomings which they find in corporate annual reports. Approximately 80 per cent of the analysts cited failure of companies to provide sales and earnings breakdowns for major product and market segments. In view of the evident importance accorded this subject by analysts participating in the study, additional questioning was employed to bring out uses which would be made of such information if available and also to ascertain how well the respondents understood the nature and inherent limitations of segment financial data. These uses are described below:

(1) *Segment reports are wanted to provide knowledge of what businesses a company is in and the relative size of the several components.* In years past, company names often described the business (e.g. Food Machinery Corporation) or names of founders were widely associated with specific types of business (e.g. W. R. Grace and Co. with ocean shipping). Diversification has drastically changed many of these companies and, not infrequently, names are deliberately chosen to avoid any connotation with specific fields of industry. Such changes reflect the fact that the complex interests of many businesses can no longer be meaningfully de-

7

scribed in brief terms such as a company name. Rather, an understanding of a diversified enterprise (particularly those of the conglomerate type) requires information about the component businesses.

Price-earnings multiples are affected by risk and prospects for future growth in earnings. These factors vary among different industries and markets and also change with time. For example, in recent years stocks in companies in electronics, drug, and business machines fields have commanded relatively high price-earnings multiples while stocks of railroads and meat packers have sold at lower multiples. Markets such as foreign countries with unstable currencies, and sales of military equipment, tend to be more volatile than domestic markets for widely used consumer goods. In the absence of information about the composition of a company's business, analysts and investors may make erroneous evaluations of its investment worth. This is evidenced by the following comments made by security analysts participating in the study.

"Some diversified companies have divisions in industries that should be worth ten times earnings, others worth 30 times. Analysts can't arrive at a proper earnings multiple for the aggregate company without knowledge of the proportions."

"This firm was asked to underwrite an issue of stock in a company carrying a name indicating that its field was electronics. Officers of the company expressed opinion that the shares should command a price-earnings multiple then current for stocks of successful electronics companies. However, investigation by the underwriter showed that a major portion of the company's sales volume was in industries whose stocks were selling at considerably lower price-earnings multiples and the electronics division was unprofitable. While the company had described its products in reports to stockholders, it had not previously disclosed the composition of sales or profits by major sources."

Information about the make-up of a business is also useful to an investor in seeking a desired balance in his portfolio. Lacking such information, an investor may unknowingly maintain too large a commitment in some one field of industry or he may pass up investment opportunities because he fails to understand and evaluate them correctly in the light of his own objectives.

Security analysts interviewed generally agreed that they are seriously handicapped in their efforts to predict earnings by most companies' nondisclosure of earnings and sometimes of sales for segments of diversified businesses. These analysts commonly estimate sales and, less often, earnings by major segments when this information is not disclosed by a company. In some instances, publicly available trade statistics provide the basic data for sales estimates which are sufficiently accurate for investors' purposes. In other instances, various other sources are utilized as illustrated in the following quotations from several analysts' reports.

> "Based on an analysis of the financial statements, discussion with the company, visits with and analysis of several of its competitors, we have attempted to estimate gross income by major activity. The results of our calculations are presented below. Even though they are subject to a wide margin of error, they might prove useful to the reader in indicating trends. Most of the figures used in the balance of the study are our own estimates."

> "We estimate that the 1966 sales breakdown will be roughly as follows: Confections, 24%, Baby Foods 23%, Catering and Feeding 22%, Beverages 15%, Pies 6%, Cocoa and Chocolate 6%, Cosmetics 4%, and Boxes under 1%. It is not possible to break down the profit contribution of each division but the Confections group has a substantially higher profit margin than other product groups."

> "While management does not give a divisional sales breakdown, it is believed that this division accounts for 50% of the company's volume and 80% of the current backlog of $35 millions."

Estimates are quite frequently confirmed as at least not misleading by company executives in private conversations with analysts. In other instances few relevant data are available and the accuracy of estimates is unknown. The investor who must depend upon analysts for such information is ordinarily unable to determine how reliable the information is.

(2) *Sales and contributions to enterprise profit are wanted in forecasting consolidated profits.* Earnings are the source of return to the stockholder on his investment and consequently profit expectations dominate investment decisions. Hence the overriding objective of the security analyst is to forecast income per share. Earnings forecasts for the current and coming year are virtually always presented in the analysis of a company's securities. These forecasts are generally expressed in dollars per share, given either as a specific number or as a range. Longer term forecasts covering periods of 2-5 years usually are limited to the expected trend with rate of change expressed in qualitative terms.

In making short-term earnings forecasts, analysts follow procedures which are closely similar though necessarily less detailed than those employed by a company's financial planning staff. Forecasting begins with the external economic environment to establish the probable demand for a company's products, the price outlook, and expected changes in operating costs. The economic outlook is not the same for all industries and forecasts need to be made for each industry in which a company has a major participation. By

9

application of its expected market shares, sales by industry for the specific company are determined. These are, in turn, converted into income with the use of margins with adjustment for expected cost changes. The basic historical information used for such forecasting procedures is a breakdown of sales and income margins for product or market segments which respond differently to changes in economic conditions and which have a material effect on consolidated earnings. In the absence of such information, the analyst or investor can make earnings forecasts for diversified companies only by projecting consolidated historical totals without consideration to the mix of different businesses included. In practice, analysts often estimate sales and profit margins for major segments and attempt to confirm the reasonableness of their estimates by questioning company officers.

(3) *A few analysts list, as another use for segment data, appraisal of the success which management of a company (particularly a conglomerate company) has had in making acquisitions.* A company which published its own financial reports usually ceases to report as a separate entity when it is acquired by another company, even though it may continue to operate with a considerable degree of autonomy. Some analysts view these subsidiary companies as segments of a parent for which separate reporting of sales and profits would be helpful.

Analysts also stated that segment margins, over a period of time, give an indication of a diversified company's management's success in its program of growth by acquisitions or internal development. Otherwise, unsuccessful ventures may be masked by consolidation with profitable segments.

Intercompany Comparisons of Segment Earnings

Contrary to opinions voiced by many company executives, those analysts interviewed stated that they do not expect to make intercompany comparisons of segment earnings. In other words, the intent is not to compare X Company's chemical division with Y Company's chemical devision because the analysts interviewed are well aware that a variety of considerations (e.g. diverse products, operating methods, organizations) render these figures noncomparable. Instead, the objective is to build up an earnings forecast for a company, segment by segment, in the same manner in which a forecast would be constructed by company personnel with historical sales and margin data at its command. No comparison of Company X with Company Y is made until the pieces have been

assembled into forecasts of consolidated earnings for each company.
Some analysts will probably make intercompany comparisons with segment data and draw invalid inferences. However, similar comparisons are made with many types of information now reported by companies. That some individuals may fail to understand the limitations does not seem to justify withholding information which has potential value to many investors.

The manner in which segment operating results will be used by skilled analysts and knowledgeable investors has important implications for the design of useful reporting techniques, as shown subsequently.

Uses in Making Bank Credit Decisions

Like shareholders, long-term creditors are strongly interested in profitability of a debtor company because, in a going concern, profits are the source of funds for paying interest and principal of loans. The bank credit analyst thus has uses for segment operating data that are closely similar to those of the security analysts.

In making short-term loan decisions, the banker tends to focus attention on short-period cash flow as a measure of a customer's ability to meet maturing financial obligations. The bank credit analyst's interest in segment operating results for short-term loans comes primarily from a desire to disclose areas of weakness such as unprofitable products or markets that absorb rather than produce funds for meeting debts.

Bankers do, of course, have power to command much more information from a customer than do investors at large. Business managers know that their bankers receive financial information in confidence and, if requests for such information are not met, the terms of a loan may be less favorable or credit may be denied. However, bankers interviewed in this study often stated that management in many small companies and even in some large companies does not have a sufficiently good financial information system to show relative profitability of major product and market segments. Even where such information is available, bankers do not always insist on receiving it, for competitive reasons.

Uses by Governmental Agencies

Although the initial demand for segment reporting came largely from security analysts, pressure for action has emanated from governmental agencies which, by virtue of existing and potential laws, have power to compel companies to report on segment operations. Thus, in April 1965, the Senate Subcommittee on

Antitrust and Monopoly conducted hearings on bills introduced by Senator Long, (S. 1842, S. 1843, S. 1844). These bills would require companies selling to affiliated and independent firms to disclose the sales, cost of sales (itemized), certain expenses, and net profit or loss. The Chairman of the Federal Trade Commission, Mr. Paul Dixon, recommended that these disclosures not be restricted to vertically integrated companies, but also include diversified companies.

In the course of testimony given at these hearings, Professor Joel Dirlam made the following statement:[9]

> "The relative profitability of different divisions and product lines should be brought out in order to appraise the competitive tactics utilizing diversification. We are operating in almost complete ignorance in this area when we do not know even the sales of many of the major firms in different lines, let alone the profitability or losses incurred in these lines. We cannot reach a judgment which is supportable in proposing legislation or changes in public policy."

The preceding quotation suggests that certain legislative and administrative authorities would use segment financial data to measure growth and concentration of various companies' shares of the market for selected products and areas.

Types of segment information desired by agencies concerned with antitrust, legislation and administration of such legislation have been indicated in a paper by John M. Blair, Chief Economist, Senate Antitrust and Monopoly Subcommittee and described more concretely in discussion of this paper at the Tulane University Symposium on public reporting on product line information.[10] In essence, each company would be expected to provide a breakdown of sales and profits for three-digit classifications in the U.S. Bureau of the Budget's Standard Industrial Classification. Such data supposedly would enable economists to measure the degree of concentration in sales for product classifications and to study changes in these figures. The data might also throw light on realization of economies or diseconomies of size among producers of various products and possible existence of unfair competitive practices. Validity and usefulness of these data for the intended purposes was not explored in this study and is not discussed here.

Objectives of these government agencies and the uses they would make of segment operating data are obviously quite different from the purposes and uses of investors and creditors. As a consequence,

---

[9] Hearings, Subcommittee on Antitrust and Monopoly, Committee on the Judiciary, United States Senate, Eighty-Ninth Congress, First Session, p. 769.

[10] See proceedings to be published in Spring 1968 by Prentice-Hall, Inc.

the types of information needed are also different. The Standard Industrial Classification was designed for use in collecting certain types of economic statistics rather than for separating an individual company into segments useful for forecasting profits and understanding its activities. Neither would application of the SIC enable valid comparisons to be made between different companies. To illustrate:[11]

> "A company manufacturing a complete line of autos and trucks would receive a single four-digit number; a company that manufactures a certain combination of parts less than a total automobile would find itself with two or more classifications. The same is true of aircraft and aircraft parts and of different types of retail operations."

For reasons described in a subsequent chapter, the extensive use of arbitrary allocations which would be required to produce net income figures for such classifications would render the data virtually meaningless in many companies.

In conclusion, evidence assembled in this study indicates rather clearly that needs for segment data expressed by investors and by government authorities concerned with anti-trust matters are distinctly different. Segment data desired by the latter group could not serve investors and creditors effectively. In the remainder of this report, attention is directed exclusively to reports for information of investors and creditors.

Reactions by Company Executives

Needs for information expressed by users of financial reports and the sympathetic attitude taken by the SEC had convinced virtually all company executives participating in this study that disclosure of segment sales and earnings will eventually be required of all companies subject to SEC regulations. Most company executives also recognize the various users' needs, but are not certain as to precisely what information is required, how to overcome the technical accounting problems, and what constraints are suitable to prevent the disclosure of information which may be damaging to the company and its stockholders. Among company executives interviewed, statements such as the following were made frequently.

> "From a single kind of business, this company has diversified until it now operates in ten widely different fields. Financial analysts don't have a good understanding of the company because most of those we see are specialists in specific industries. They just don't get the picture when they deal with a conglomerate company."

> "This company is difficult to understand because of the combinations

---

[11] Robert K. Mautz, "Bases for More Detailed Reporting by Diversified Companies," *Financial Executive*, November 1967, p. 54.

of different types of business that have occurred. Management feels that is has an obligation to provide stockholders with reports that are informative and pertinent. These reports should tell what types of businesses the company is in and where its revenues come from. Hence, its reports have been designed to tell what the major components of the business are and to give their relative importance."

The intent of this study is to throw light on the subject through presenting pertinent factual information and analysis. Based on this analysis, certain suggestions are formulated with respect to the directions segment reporting might take.

CHAPTER 2

Technical Problems in Segment Reporting

SUMMARY

Important technical problems which arise in preparing financial reports for segments of a business are (1) selecting the segments for which to report, and (2) measuring segment revenues and costs. Uses which suppliers of capital make of segment reports are guides to resolution of these problems.

For making forecasts of future income, a diversified business needs to be divided into segments, each of which is relatively homogeneous in its response to economic conditions. In most instances groups of end-products are the significant segments, but in some cases market segments replace or supplement product segments. Differences in company operations preclude meaningful application of any uniform classification of segments to all companies. Consequently, it is essential that users of segment reports build up a forecast of aggregate earnings for each company and limit intercompany comparisons to consolidated earnings.

Presence of both joint revenues and joint costs makes it impossible to determine net profit for individual segments except with arbitrary allocations which tend to render segment figures invalid as measures of contributions to aggregate enterprise earnings. Where a company's operations are highly integrated, it may be possible to segregate sales of major-end products, but reliable segment profit margins cannot be determined. Such a company must be viewed as a single unit in forecasting earnings. Where there is a lesser degree of jointness in revenues and costs, as there is in companies composed of segments linked together principally by centralized administrative and financial functions, segment contributions to common costs and profit can be reliable and useful for forecasting aggregate enterprise earnings.

IMPORTANT TECHNICAL PROBLEMS must be met and satisfactorily solved in order to prepare useful financial reports for segments of a business. While they are interrelated and must be considered together in practice, these problems are discussed below under two headings.

1. Selecting the segments for which to report to outsiders.
2. Measuring segment revenues and cost.

Security and credit analysts are not skilled in accounting practice and, with a few exceptions, individuals interviewed did not propose specific techniques for producing reports to meet the needs they described for information about segment operations.[1] On the other hand, as experts, accountants should be able to devise measurement and reporting techniques to provide users of accounting reports with information relevant to their needs.

Both company executives who participated in the study and many writers on the subject have placed emphasis on the technical difficulties that will be encountered in preparing reliable segment reports. Some persons view the difficulties as impossible to overcome and oppose disclosure of segment operating results as inherently unreliable in the hands of outsiders. There are important problems to be solved and the reports which will emerge are likely to be somewhat different from consolidated reports now used by

---

[1] This is not to say that interviewees were not knowledgeable about accounting and skilled in the use of accountants' reports. Some analysts had had experience as well as education in accounting and one held a CPA certificate.

investors and creditors. Hence these groups will need to learn to use segment reports effectively.

SELECTING SEGMENTS FOR WHICH TO REPORT

Discussions of segment reporting have been marked by much confusion over identification and definition of the segments of a company for which external financial reports are proposed. Uncritical use of terms such as product line and divisional reporting have tended to obscure the fact that selection of company subdivisions for which to report is one of the major questions which must be resolved in devising useful reporting procedures. The word *segment* is used in this report to designate any reporting entity which is a subdivision of a larger business. Such usage facilitates discussion, in general terms, of problems of reporting for various subdivisions without limitations connoted by specific terms like division, product, market, etc. The term segment has long been used for this purpose in NAA research reports.

Uses for Information as Guides to Segment Selection

Inability to resolve the question of for what segments to report is traceable to failure to first establish clearly the uses which investors and creditors would make of segment financial data. Once these uses are known, generalizations can be drawn with respect to characteristics of segments which will be relevant to report users' purposes. These generalizations can then serve as guides in selecting the segments of each business for which reports will be useful to investors and creditors.

The initial step in this NAA study was to learn specifically how financial and credit analysts would use operating results for segments of a business. As stated in Chapter 1, the findings from this phase of the study were that the important uses would be to provide an understanding of the sources of a diversified company's earnings and to build up forecasts of consolidated earnings. In this latter process, a separate forecast of the contribution to aggregate earnings is made for each segment subject to a distinctive set of economic factors.

> To illustrate, a company produces drugs, chemical fibers, and industrial machinery. Market conditions and factors affecting production costs for these three segments of the company's business sometimes differ and prospective earnings trends diverge. The analyst needs to know contributions to company sales and earnings for each of these product groups in order to translate forecasts of the economic outlook for each group into an earnings forecast.

17

In other instances, the significant segments of a company's business may be markets rather than products.

> To illustrate, a company produces containers of numerous types, made of different materials (glass, plastic, metal, paper, etc.) and by different processes. A broad line of these containers is sold in markets, each of which have distinctively different characteristics. Internal forecasting and reporting is structured by markets rather than by products. Company executives expressed the opinion that sales and margins for these markets would also be helpful to investors, but that a similar breakdown by product classifications would be virtually useless.
>
> Another company makes and sells a number of food products both in the United States and in another country whose currency may be devalued in the near future. In order to estimate the probable impact devaluation would have on the company's earnings for the coming year, it is essential to know what portion of consolidated sales and earnings are drawn from the country in question.

Much discussion of segment reporting has been fruitless because participants have implicitly assumed that some uniform classification of segments (e.g., the Standard Industrial Classification) could be used by all companies or prescribed by some authoritative group. Reflection and discussion with interviewees in all three groups led to the conclusion that it is very unlikely that any uniform classification of segments based on industry or product characteristics can either reduce unlike companies to comparable terms or provide investors with significant operating results for subdivisions of individual companies. The best results are likely to be obtained by reporting for those segments of each company which best meet the needs for segment information described in Chapter 1 of this report. Management has the requisite knowledge of company operations for selecting segments to be reported on, but it needs to acquaint itself with and be guided by uses which investment and credit analysts wish to make of segment operating results.

Materiality of Segments

Another guide for distinguishing a significant segment for external reporting is that the segment should make a material contribution to consolidated sales and earnings. Thus the SEC has set 15 per cent as the materiality threshold above which segment contributions to gross volume of business must be disclosed by companies registering securities.[2] However, the concept of materiality is a subjective one and any specific measure such as the foregoing 15 per cent of total gross revenues is necessarily arbitrary.

The arbitrary nature of such a standard of materiality implies

---

[2] Form S-1, item 9; Form 10, item 3.

need for some flexibility in its application. Where disclosure of segment results may bring a damaging reaction from competitors, customers, or governments, the disclosure burden obviously falls harder on a small company than a large one which, merely because its total sales are larger, may be excused from disclosure for some segments. Moreover, a management that wishes to avoid disclosure may be able to arrange its segment groupings in such a way that some or even all segments are below the prescribed criterion. Certain comments are made subsequently on the need to consider all aspects of each situation in designing and administering a segment reporting program.

While a few investment analysts interviewed remarked that, "We want all the information we can get," each analyst ordinarily follows a number of companies and has limited time to devote to each one. Moreover, he can justify the additional time required to handle more detailed data only when a worthwhile improvement in his forecasts can thereby be made. A company often has sales and cost data for perhaps thousands of individual products because management at subordinate levels makes decisions about each item. On the other hand, managers responsible for overall profits work with a limited number of major segments. It seems reasonable to conclude that outsiders need no more segment detail than top management. In most instances, it seems likely that relatively few broad segments are sufficient for the investor's income forecasting purposes, provided these segments are reasonably homogeneous with respect to their response to economic influences impinging on profitability.

Divisions as Reporting Segments

In the controversy over segment reporting, reference is often made to divisions as segments for which external reports might be made. The term *division* has different meanings in different companies. Most commonly, the term denotes managerial responsibilities in a company where management has been decentralized by delegating authority for a comparatively broad range of functions to each division head. Ordinarily, a division is a separate profit responsibility encompassing authority over both sales and costs, although some functions (e.g. finance, research) remain centralized.[3] The accounting systems of such companies are

---

[3] In a functional organization, divisions constitute responsibilities for functions such as production, sales, finance, etc. Here divisions are not profit responsibilities because only central management has coordinating authority over functions which can be measured by profit margins.

usually structured to collect costs and revenues by managerial responsibilities represented by divisions and their sub-units.[4] In companies where such organization and accounting practices prevail, divisional margin figures are available and could be reported to outsiders, either before or after allocating the costs of centralized functions.

Divisions in some manufacturing companies coincide with product classifications.

> For example, Wallace & Tiernan, Inc. has three divisions—Chemical, Equipment, and Pharmaceutical—each headed by a Vice President responsible for profitability of his division. Profits are disclosed in annual reports to stockholders for each of these three divisions.

While the above represents a clear-cut situation in which company organization and accounting structure follow the same broad product groupings useful to outsiders, product lines assigned to divisions are not always homogeneous. Products with unlike characteristics are assigned to a given division for a variety of reasons such as physical contiguity of the operations, managerial competence, advantage from integrating or combining production or marketing operations, historical accident, etc. Furthermore, products and markets are frequently shifted among divisions as central management seeks more effective organization patterns or adjustment to changing conditions. In some cases, divisions are market-oriented and each division handles a variety of products in a given market. Under any of these circumstances divisions are, at best, only approximations to those segments which may be the relevant segments to investors. Different classifications which cut across divisional segments established for managerial purposes are likely to be needed to meet the needs expressed by financial analysts.

Products and Markets as Reporting Segments

Important practical problems would be encountered by many companies in preparing revenue margins for product or market segments. These problems arise because as noted previously, accounting systems are designed to measure financial performance for managerial responsibilities comprising segments of the company organization. In such companies there is commonly no provision for repetitive periodic reporting of earnings by products or markets. When product cost and margin data are wanted by

---

[4] Asset accounts are often similarly structured, but liabilities and net worth are centralized corresponding to centralization of the finance function.

management for profit planning or pricing decisions, the data are assembled by special studies.

Comments made by users of financial reports often seem to reflect the belief that costs are always accumulated by products. This impression is supported by many textbooks on cost accounting which fail to recognize that managerial planning and control is exercised through organizational responsibilities (usually termed divisions) and that modern accounting systems are designed primarily to measure managerial performance.

Company executives participating in the study frequently made comments of which the following are representative.

"A great deal of additional work and expense would be required to report regularly by product lines because this company's system is designed to produce costs and margins by managerial responsibilities rather than by products. But it would be possible to do the job by special analysis once a year."

"It takes us several months to work out product costs for internal planning purposes."

"We have never had profit and loss reports by products. The books collect profits by organizational responsibilities. Reporting by product classifications would be a real problem for us."

"For internal reporting, we recognize three profit responsibilities which represent sales by different customer industries. These are not homogeneous, for they contain products which fluctuate in different ways with market conditions. Through our computer installation, progress is being made toward better sales classification in terms of markets."

In a number of companies, interviewees stated that development of computer-based accounting systems will eventually facilitate cross-classification of sales and costs, but that this entails some additional expense.

Review of evidence from this study leads to the conclusion that no single segment classification pattern can be applied to all companies. Wide differences in company operations make it necessary to select, in each case, the segments which will be useful to investors in understanding a company's business and in forecasting the outlook for earnings in future periods. As noted above, the useful segments are product groups in some cases, markets in other cases. There are also companies where at least some breakdowns into both product and market segments are needed.

The primary characteristic which makes a segment significant to investors and creditors is homogeneity in the effect of economic conditions on earnings. The determining condition is that analysts need to have separate sales and margin figures for a segment in order to understand the business, to make forecasts of consolidated profit, and to appraise management's diversification strategy. On the other hand, security analysts have no need for further subdivisions of a segment which can be handled as a homogeneous unit for the preceding purposes. Also there is no need to separate segments which are not material in size.

In some companies, divisions coincide reasonably well with segment classifications relevant to analysts' purposes; in other companies the needed segment classifications cut across existing divisions.

MEASURING SEGMENT REVENUES AND COSTS

The fact that products, markets, and divisions are not separate businesses but instead are integral parts of a single enterprise makes it impossible to determine net profit figures which are fully valid measures of individual segment performance. The underlying reason is that some portion of the costs and sometimes a portion of the revenues can be separated only by arbitrary actions which may have usefulness for some purposes but tend to reduce the reliability of segment cost and revenue data for forecasting future earnings.

During comparatively recent years, important developments have taken place in accounting techniques for providing management with reliable information for evaluating the contributions of individual segments to aggregate profit. These techniques are particularly useful in forecasting and profit planning. Findings in this study suggest that the same techniques can be adapted to serve the needs expressed by investors and creditors for segment data relevant to forecasting enterprise income.

Since many users of financial reports, including some accountants, do not fully understand the nature and significance of joint costs and revenues, these are briefly discussed below in the context of segment reporting. In subsequent pages and the following chapter, reporting techniques employing different approaches to joint cost problems are described.

Characteristics of Joint Costs and Revenues

A joint cost is incurred as a lump sum expenditure for a combination of output units representing groups of sales dollars from different products or markets. The diverse units are produced together rather than separately because joint production is more profitable than separate production. Thus the motivating force leading to joint output is economic.[5]

From the standpoint of this study, the significant characteristic of a joint cost situation is that the individual segments in a combination have no separate costs. While accountants allocate joint costs in a variety of ways, all of their procedures are essentially arbitrary. Allocations are rationalized by assumptions with respect to how the several segments in a joint combination share benefits provided by the cost. However, it is impossible to verify any of these assumptions. Equally competent accountants may arrive at quite different segment costs by choosing different allocation methods and there is no way to prove that any one set of figures is correct to exclusion of the others. Apportionments of joint costs are useful for certain managerial purposes (for example, in planning how joint cost is to be recovered in pricing), but any material amount of allocated joint cost destroys the usefulness of a segment profit margin for forecasting or appraising segment contribution to consolidated profit.

A characteristic of all arbitrary allocations is that they lack universality. Sooner or later circumstances arise in which allocation procedures break down and yield misleading or even absurd results.

> For example, a change in the number of allocation basis units recorded for one product in a joint combination (due to change in some factor such as labor rates, production volume or selling price) may alter the proportions in which joint costs are shared among the products with repercussions on profits ascribed to other products. Not infrequently one segment in a joint combination shows a loss under accounting methods employed although to abandon the "unprofitable" segment would reduce aggregate earnings from the group. Segment reports which show such situations are meaningless and possibly misleading.

The only guides available for choosing allocation procedures are subjective tests described by terms such as "equity" and "reasonableness." When one procedure goes awry, the accountant changes the allocation basis to get results judged more acceptable.

The problem raised by joint costs cannot be solved by establishing uniform allocation methods to be used by all companies because this would not avoid the arbitrary determination of costs

---

[5] It is always possible to produce separately rather than jointly but may be less profitable. For example, the natural gas which accompanies liquid petroleum is sometimes discarded where transportation to a market is unprofitable. See *Costing Joint Products*, NAA Research Report 31; W. B. McFarland, *Concepts for Management Accounting*, National Association of Accountants, 1966, Chapter 3.

which causes segment margin to be invalid as measures of segment contributions to company profit.

Revenues as well as costs may be joint, for aggregate revenue from selling products together is not infrequently greater than it would be if they were sold separately. This appears seldom to be a serious problem in measuring segment results for investors' and creditors' purposes so long as sales are made to outsiders. In an integrated company where a substantial part of sales by some segments is internal, it is impossible to ascribe revenues to individual segments except by arbitrary procedures which tend to vitiate reliability of the data for forecasting profits.

Prices drawn from an outside market are often not realistic measures of segment contributions to aggregate enterprise revenues. Reasons for this were explained by an executive of a large petroleum company:

> "For certain internal purposes, a breakdown between production and refining can be made using market transfer prices for crude oil. These prices would be valid in a small company because small quantities could be bought or sold at these prices. For this company these prices are not valid because it could not sell the large quantities in the market. In my view, it is neither useful nor possible to break down income by parts of a large integrated oil company.
> "On the other hand, income from our chemical operations can be separated because reliable market prices exist for the materials and the joint portion of total cost of the products is minor. We report sales for these products but do not disclose profit for competitive reasons."

Integrated operations are not restricted to classic joint product industries such as petroleum refining.

> For example, a manufacturer of animal feeds entered the production of poultry on a large scale in order to protect its market for feeds. To discontinue the poultry operation would have reduced aggregate profit by considerably more than the separable profit attributable to poultry production. To break out a separate profit on poultry production was viewed as meaningless by company representatives because the operation was solely a way of marketing feed.

In such circumstances, segments which appear to be readily separable when viewed superficially are found to be integrated when management's objectives are explored. When the integration is limited, a marked difference in the operations carried on exists, and separate organizational units are employed (e.g. subsidiary corporations), there is a greater tendency to report separately, both internally and externally. Following are two examples.

> A large manufacturing company acquired an insurance company in order to obtain savings in insurance costs. Finding the insurance business offered an attractive return on its investment, the company expanded its insurance operation. Company executives stated that investors

should receive separate reports for the insurance subsidiary because of the wide differences in nature of the business.

A retail merchandising company established a subsidiary finance company to handle its customer installment accounts. Company executives explained that return on investment in the finance subsidiary was lower than in merchandising but credit facilities had a beneficial effect on sales and profits of retail stores. While this effect could not be measured and credited to the finance subsidiary, interviewees felt that differences in the operations justified disclosure.

Limitations to Segment Reporting Where Revenues and Costs are Joint

If joint revenues or costs are relatively insignificant in amount, arbitrary allocations will not have a serious effect on usefulness of segment sales and profit margins to investment and credit analysts. These conditions are most likely to obtain where segments are virtually self-contained businesses sharing only centralized administrative and financing functions. Such companies tend to be more like investment companies than operating companies. Whether or not allocated, analysts wish to have the amount of joint central headquarters costs disclosed. One financial analyst remarked that, "In such circumstances the analyst can allocate the common costs as well as the accountant can if he has any reason to want segment net profits on an all-in basis."

However, even though joint costs are not significant in relation to sales, they are often material in relation to profit. For example, in one company where joint corporate headquarters costs amounted to only 15% of consolidated sales, these costs were 34.2% of consolidated net income. Under such conditions, the allocation method chosen can have an important effect on the apparent profitability of individual segments. Reliable segment sales figures can be reported in many cases where meaningful segment net profits cannot be ascertained. As explained in Chapter 3, figures which serve analysts' major needs can also be provided by reporting segment margins before deducting common costs from the aggregate segment margin.[6]

At the opposite extreme, where operations are closely integrated, it is virtually impossible to produce operating statements which are valid measures of the individual segments' contributions to the whole business. The reason is that the results reported for each segment reflect only arbitrary actions taken in allocating joint revenues and costs rather than performance of the segments. These technical barriers to determining meaningful segment mar-

---

[6] For an example, see 1966 Annual Report, National Distillers and Chemical Corp.

gins are not shortcomings in accounting techniques because accountants cannot be expected to make separate measurements when operations are organized in such a manner that separate revenues and costs do not exist.

This situation does not handicap analysts because operating results for individual segments of an integrated business would have no usefulness in making investment decisions. The entire series of integrated operations must be performed before any revenue can accrue to the enterprise. For example, an integrated oil company must not only produce, but it must also refine, transport, and market its products before it realizes any income. Nothing would be accomplished by attempting to make separate forecasts of the individual functions' contributions to overall profits. Rather, forecasts need to treat as a single unit all operations up to the point where end products are sold to outsiders. While a company may utilize internal transfer prices for managerial purposes (e.g. for measuring managerial performance, make-or-buy decisions), these prices are eliminated in consolidation and have no effect on the end results with which investors and creditors are concerned.

A variety of situations arise which fall between the extremes where segments either closely resemble independent businesses or are nonseparable parts of an integrated whole:

1. Costs may be joint up to a split-off point after which costs and revenues are separable. For example, raw materials used by the petrochemical division of an oil company are jointly produced with other petroleum products. For internal profitability measurements the company determines the margin of chemical products revenue over separable cost, although this margin is not disclosed to outsiders for competitive reasons. In general, such margins are valid measures of segment contribution to consolidated profits and would be useful to analysts. Significance of contribution margins of this type will be greater where the excluded joint cost is relatively small because variations in the margin will then have greater impact on consolidated profits. Where there is little separable cost, real question arises as to the justification for separate reporting. Contribution margins as measures of segment profit ability are described in the following chapter.

2. Both sales to outsiders and transfers to subsequent operations may be made at various stages in an integrated series of operations. When outside sales are relatively minor, the segments are best reported on as a single unit because realistic transfer prices do not exist. For example, an automobile engine plant sells a few engines to outsiders but transfers most of its production to assembly lines. On the other hand, when outside sales are significant, separate reporting with internal transfers accounted for at market prices seems desirable in order to disclose the size and importance of the segments in the total company business. To illustrate, the packaging division of one company obtains

a large volume of plastics from a subsidiary which also has large outside sales. Transfer prices employed are viewed by management as realistic opportunity costs. Reporting only on a consolidated basis, with intracompany sales eliminated, would not show the size of the plastics operation. Executives expressed opinion that such disclosure is important to understand the business and for making forecasts of future earnings.

Segments of a diversified business always share some resources in common with the consequence that some costs and often some revenues are joint. This precludes any possibility of determining fully independent segment net profit figures because the segments are not independent businesses. The additional (or possibly lesser) profit which arises from the synergistic effects of combination can be treated in either of two ways:

1. By allocating it among the segments in some unavoidably arbitrary manner through allocation of joint costs and revenues.
2. By showing the results of synergy only in the consolidated profit after charging segments only with separable revenues and costs.

Where jointness of costs and revenues is a significant factor, as it probably is in most diversified companies, the first method seriously reduces the validity of reported segment results and also the usefulness of the figures for purposes of investment and credit analysis. The second method yields more useful results but has not been widely used in public reporting with the result that some education of report users probably is needed to insure understanding.

The influence of external economic conditions on selection of segments for reporting was discussed in the first section of this chapter. Here it was stated that analysts need information about only those segments which are affected by distinctly different economic conditions and that each segment reported on should be reasonably homogeneous in that it is affected by the same economic conditions. Internal organization for operation also has an important influence on the question of for what segments to prepare separate reports. Where operations are highly integrated, it is neither possible to produce meaningful separate earnings figures, nor would such figures be useful. Segment reports are more reliable and most useful when activities of each segment are, to a high degree, separable and self-contained.

Finally, in preparing and using operating results for segments of a business, it must be kept in mind that they cannot be equivalent to operating results for independent businesses.

27

CHAPTER 3

Contribution Margin Reporting

SUMMARY

This chapter describes contribution margin techniques and how they might be used in external reporting for segments in order to avoid arbitrary allocations of joint costs.

Segment contribution margin is the excess of segment revenue over separable costs of the segment. It measures each segment's contribution to common corporate costs and aggregate profit. The term seems preferable to a qualified profit because the latter may have misleading connotations.

Effective forecasting of segment contribution margins requires analysis of segment costs according to their behavior in a segment's profit structure. Disclosure of sufficient detail to enable users of financial reports to distinguish variable, annual programmed, and long-run capacity costs is suggested.

Interviews showed that investment and credit analysts would find contribution margin reporting for segments very useful in terms of their work. Company executives often questioned the feasibility of the method, although this attitude sometimes reflected misunderstanding and unawareness that similar procedures are used internally in many companies. Objections to disclosure of such data are considered in Chapter 7.

A CONTRIBUTION MARGIN is the addition to aggregate enterprise profit which is ascribable to the presence of a given segment in contrast to the aggregate profit which would have resulted in the absence of the segment. The contribution which each segment makes is measured in its turn under the assumption that all other segments will remain unchanged. When measured in this manner, some enterprise costs will be unassigned. These are costs of central corporate headquarters functions common to all segments. There may also be unassigned revenue from sources such as temporary investments of corporate funds, tax refunds, dividends from affiliates, and other gains not arising from operations of any individual segment. Such common costs are deducted and common revenues added to the total of the segment contribution margins in arriving at consolidated net profit. Exhibit I shows the general form in which contribution margins statements might appear. The specific form and content of such a statement would, of course, have to be developed for each company.

The term *contribution margin* seems to be a good one because it describes the measure of segment performance desired and it has been widely used in the literature on management accounting. While the term is unfamiliar to many investors, bankers, and analysts, the concept is relatively simple and, with some explanation in the financial reports where it appears, it should be readily understood. It seems preferable to avoid the word profit because it carries connotations which may be misleading when applied to a segment margin from which some costs have not been deducted.

APPLICATION OF CONTRIBUTION MARGIN REPORTING TO EXTERNAL REPORTING

Contribution margin reporting proceeds by assigning to each segment the revenues and costs for which that segment is solely responsible. These are, in other words, the separable revenues and costs. A practical test is that the separable costs would not be

29

EXHIBIT I

Segment Contributions to Company Profit*
(000 omitted)

	Segment A	Segment B	Segment C	Totals
Sales	$300,000	$200,000	$500,000	$1,000,000
Separable Segment Costs:				
Materials, supplies, and services				
Wages, salaries, employee benefits		(Details omitted)		
Insurance, property taxes ...				
Depreciation				
Advertising and selling expenses				
Totals	245,000	187,500	407,500	840,000
Segment Contribution to Corporate Common Costs and Profit	55,000	12,500	92,500	160,000
Corporate Common Costs:				
Administration				
Research and development..		(Details omitted)		
Interest on borrowed funds.				
Income tax				
Total				80,000
Net Profit				$ 80,000

*Adapted from McFarland, *Concepts for Management Accounting*, National Association of Accountants, 1966, p. 69.

present in the absence of the segment in question with all other conditions remaining the same. A long-run point of view needs to be taken in applying this test. That is, the situation should be viewed as it would be after all plant and equipment used in the specific segment's operations have been disposed of or transferred to other uses. Costs of facilities such as central headquarters shared jointly with other segments need not be allocated unless items of material size in these costs will be affected by changing fortunes of the individual segment.

Expansion or contraction of one segment often has repercussions on revenues and costs of other segments. Unless these are of such size that they have a material effect on an outsider's view of segment operations, such interrelationships may be ignored in external reporting. Analysts' forecasts of future earnings per share for the company are not likely to be highly sensitive to minor imprecision in measuring segment costs. If operations of two or more segments are so closely integrated that major amounts of revenue or cost are nonseparable, they usually should, as stated in Chapter 2, be treated as a single unit for external reporting.

In the preceding chapter, contribution margins were suggested for measuring segment profitability where joint costs make it impossible to arrive at segment net profit figures which are meaningful and useful. This is an application of the economist's marginal analysis which is widely employed by management for projecting changes in segment profits when profit planning decisions are being made. Contribution margin techniques and how they might be used in external reporting for segments of a business are discussed in this chapter.

Since there is little practice, the material presented is largely the result of analysis and reasoning. However, many companies use contribution margin techniques for internal reporting on segment operations and these methods provide general guidance for developing possible external reporting methods.[1] Working methods and comments by analysts provide support for conclusions derived by analysis.

The more familiar costing methods used in accounting assign costs to units on the basis of benefits received, measuring these benefits by assumptions where the flow cannot be traced, and leaving no cost undistributed. In contrast, the contribution margin approach assigns costs on the basis of direct causal responsibility and leaves unassigned those costs which are incurred for the business as a whole.

When all items specific to individual segments have been assigned to their respective segments, the margin after deducting each segment's costs from its revenues measures the separable contribution which it has made to the common unassigned costs and profit. To allocate the common corporate costs among segments may be helpful for motivating managers responsible for internal profit centers to recover these costs. However, outsiders do not have such managerial responsibility and are interested only in identifiable segment contributions, unobscured by subjective

---

[1] For a description of these methods, see McFarland, *Concepts for Management Accounting,* National Association of Accountants, 1966, Chapter 3.

allocations of items which are irrelevant to the making of profit projections.

Segment Detail Useful to Analysts

It was shown earlier that a major aspect of security analysts' work is forecasting earnings and analysts contend that, for a diversified company, forecasts must be built up by individual segments. In doing this as best he can from the information available, the analyst estimates how the separable revenues and costs of each major segment will change under the economic conditions which he expects to prevail. Thus, beginning with revenues, he adjusts the most recent sales figures available to reflect the effects of anticipated changes in selling prices and sales volumes. As noted in Chapter 2, better forecasts can be made if the segments are homogeneous in the sense that revenues from products grouped together tend to respond in the same manner to changes in market conditions.

The next step is to project costs for each segment. To do this effectively, analysts need a sufficiently detailed classification of costs to identify the key elements in each segment's cost structure. Leaving aside the question of how much detail can be disclosed without having the data used by outsiders to the company's detriment,[2] the following information about costs is generally relevant to investment and credit analysts' purposes.

Projecting Segment Costs

Three types of costs need to be distinguished in forecasting segment contribution margins because these costs behave somewhat differently as conditions change. In the first group are *variable costs*, the total of which tends to vary in direct proportion to production or sales activity. Given information shown in Exhibit I, the analyst would usually view the first two items under separable segment costs as variable costs. While this assumption may not be completely true for items such as employment costs, the relatively large sales increments dealt with by analysts are likely to cause some change in the number of salaried employees (i.e., supervisors, clerks, engineers, etc.) as well as in hourly labor. Where a company has ascertained the amount of its short-run variable costs for internal planning and control, disclosure of such information would be helpful to the analyst.

A second group of costs is comprised of *programmed costs* which

---

[2] This topic is considered in Chapter 6.

are budgeted annually in amounts determined by planned activity programs such as advertising, selling, employee training and research and development carried out at the segment level. While some of the expenditures planned for these activities are intended to produce revenues in the coming year (e.g., direct selling), others are in effect investments which are expected to have a longer pay-off period. For example, in one company management believed that the market for a product offered attractive opportunities for growth. Hence it budgeted comparatively large expenditures to carry out a market development program extending over several years with knowledge that these expenditures would substantially reduce near-term profits from the product. Such information throws valuable light on the financial results reported from period to period.

Skilled analysts usually attempt to supplement the information disclosed in published reports by questioning management about its plans for activities which are the source of programmed costs. However, management is in a position to know what additional information is needed to understand the effect which these costs are likely to have on future segment margins and, if management takes responsibility for disclosing pertinent information, its company's investment worth is more likely to be fairly evaluated in the financial markets. As a minimum, analysts consider it essential that disclosure be made of amounts spent for such purposes as advertising, selling, and research wherever these activities are an important aspect of a segment's operations.

The final group of segment costs comprises costs such as depreciation, property taxes, and insurance which originate in long period commitments of capital in the form of plant and equipment. These costs represent capacity to produce, but within the limits of existing capacity the amounts of cost change little in total with increments in output. Where a company's cost structure includes a large proportion of such costs, an increase in sales tends to produce a disproportionate change in profits. For this reason, disclosure of the amount of relatively fixed costs must be made if the analyst is to make reliable forecasts of income.

While not variable with output, these long-run capacity costs change in total from year to year under the influence of factors such as plant additions, changes in tax rates, and accounting methods. Hence supplementary information about new facilities, depreciation methods, etc., is needed by making income forecasts. Analysts use published sources of various types for clues to cost changes and seek to supplement and confirm such information by questioning company managements.

Applications of expense classifications suggested in Exhibit I will require judgment, but not to a degree exceeding that now widely employed and accepted in accounting practice. For example, the classification of costs as inventoriable or non-inventoriable and the distinction between charges to be capitalized or expensed requires exercise of judgment, both in establishing each company's rules and in applying these rules. Expense classifications in segment statements need not be highly precise unless it is found that forecasts of earnings per share are very sensitive to minor errors in expense classification. Organization of the data in a manner relevant to the analyst's purposes is likely to be more important than a high degree of accuracy. Disclosure of groups of costs which tend to behave in the same manner is also likely to be more useful than extensive itemization of costs.

PRESENT PRACTICE IN USE OF CONTRIBUTION MARGIN ANALYSIS

Most published income statements disclose totals for depreciation and depletion, although there are usually substantial amounts of other operating costs (e.g. property taxes, insurance) which are not variable with ordinary short-run changes in output. Nevertheless, an approximation to the marginal income ratio can be calculated for those companies that disclose sufficient detail of their operating costs. This ratio measures the rate at which operating profit increases per dollar of sales. Analysts interviewed reported that such estimates can be made more successfully for certain companies (most of which are concentrated in a few industries) than for other companies. These companies disclose operating costs in more detail and also commonly do not defer long-run fixed costs such as depreciation in inventory. Because of the latter practice, changes in inventory have less tendency to obscure the relationship between volume and profits.

The foregoing estimates are, of course, based on consolidated income statement data. From study of the economic outlook for specific industries and through discussion with company executives, the analyst then seeks to obtain an indication of the expected trends in sales, costs, and prices for major product lines. If he has been able to obtain information about the profit structure of the product lines, he traces the effect of previously ascertained trends on segment contributions to company profits.

In the absence of any knowledge of segment contribution mar-

34

gins, the analyst is compelled to project consolidated profit by using historical ratios of consolidated profit to sales. This approach is likely to result in wide margins of error when applied to diversified companies having product lines or other segments with varying contribution margin ratios.

The following excerpts from analysts' reports illustrate applications of procedures described above. A somewhat more extensive use of projected cost-profit-volume relationships in an analyst's report is illustrated in Exhibit II.

"In common with other steel manufacturers, there exists a high degree of leverage in the company's cost structure. For estimating purposes it can be assumed that the company's incremental profit on sales at the current operating rate of 85% of capacity will be 40% or more before taxes. At operating rates below 50% and above 95%, the profit margin will be somewhat lower, reflecting shorter production runs and the higher cost of overtime labor."

"The company has a highly leveraged capital structure with net interest charges running about 15% of operating earnings. These fixed expenses, as well as the relatively fixed nature of depreciation, engineering and selling, general and administrative expenses (about 19% of sales), make earnings quite sensitive to small volume changes."

"We estimate that sales for the fiscal year ending February 28, 1967 will rise by around 35% to approximately $46 million. Reported earnings for fiscal 1966 were after an effective Federal tax rate of 17%, compared with nil for fiscal 1965, due to tax loss carry-forward. We estimate that with the help of the improved fortunes of H-K and higher margins in other divisions, pre-tax earnings should rise at a faster rate than sales. Allowing for the fact that earnings will be taxed at the full 48% in the current year, we estimate fiscal 1967 earnings at about $2 per share."

Reactions of Security Analysts to Contribution Margin Reporting

An income statement prepared on a contribution margin basis was submitted to each security analyst interviewed. These individuals were then asked to evaluate this form of income reporting in terms of their decision needs. Without a single exception, every analyst stated that this type of income statement would be considerably more useful in terms of their information needs. Following are some typical comments:

"This would be very valuable. It would throw light on companies and divisions with high operating leverages."

"This would be ideal for analysts. We now try to get this information by reconstructing the income statement but with insufficient data often reach wrong conclusions."

"This would be much more useful than the present income statement. In effect, steel and aluminum companies provide most of this

EXHIBIT II

Use of Cost—Volume—Profit Relationships by Investment Analysts

"To estimate the possible range of profit generation of the new plant recently put into operation by this company, we have made the following calculations. In our judgment, the most likely future earnings profile points to little or no earnings contributed in 1966, and then a two or three year build-up to a maximum earnings contribution of close to $.80 a share. We feel this is conservative and realistic. It might be bettered since the capacity of this plant represents only about 5% of the current market.

Income Statement
Stockholder basis (all figures $ millions)

% Capacity	30%	50%	70%	90%	100%
Sales	$4.1	$6.8	$9.5	$12.2	$13.5
Depreciation	1.0	1.0	1.0	1.0	1.0
Fixed Costs	4.0	4.0	4.0	4.0	4.0
Variable Cost	1.4	2.4	3.3	4.3	4.7
Total Costs	$6.4	$7.4	$8.3	$ 9.3	$ 9.7
Pretax Income (Loss)	(2.3)	(0.6)	1.2	2.9	3.8
Taxes (at 50%)	—	—	0.6	1.4	1.9
Net Income (Loss)	(2.3)	(0.6)	0.6	1.5	1.9

"We feel we should accept the premise that the plant will operate over this period, although we have no basis for deciding when it will be trouble-free. The "market" is being pessimistic about the early successful operation of this venture. Our bet is that the break-in will be concluded by year-end 1965, but that sales will develop slowly.

"We have set up a projected income statement at full capacity, allocating fixed costs of $4 million, $1 million straight line depreciation, and variable costs of 35% of sales. At capacity sales of 25,000 tons at $.27 per pound are $13.5 million. Fixed cost for labor is estimated at 20% and for selling, general and administrative expenses at 11%. Raw material costs of 20% and other costs 15% are the variable costs."

Reactions of Security Analysts (*Continued*)

information. This type of data is of the essence in profit projections. It also would be helpful in break-even analysis."

"This information would be extremely valuable if we could get it. It is particularly important in heavy industries since it would provide a basis for calculating the effect of changes in operating levels and costs on profits. We try to do this now but in the absence of better data, much of our effort is guesswork."

"Contribution margin reporting would provide a much more significant tool. If corporations reported product line contribution margins, security analysts would be able to achieve a level of sophistication not now possible. Our major function is to forecast short-term profit and this is difficult without a knowledge of fixed and variable costs. We rarely prepare break-even analysis because of the absence of this kind of data."

"In estimating profits, we use a pre-tax margin applied to expected sales. This is obviously unsatisfactory. While we tend to raise or lower the pre-tax margin to take into consideration the effect of operating at higher or lower volume, without segregated fixed and variable costs, this is done on a rule-of-thumb basis."

Banker's Reactions to Contribution Margin Reporting

Among the 70 bankers interviewed, 56 strongly favored contribution margin reporting. The remaining 14 bankers, who expressed either mild approval or negative reactions, generally were unfamiliar with this form of income presentation and were reluctant to support it on first exposure without fully comprehending all of the implications. Some typical comments from those bankers who endorsed contribution margin reporting follow:

"This would be very much more useful than the traditional income statement. It permits us to more readily calculate the effect of planned use of borrowed funds. It facilitates break-even analysis which is important to bankers."

"This would be very useful; however, because of the product mix in the case of diversified companies, it would be much less useful at the corporate level than for product lines."

"Unquestionably, this would represent a valuable tool, particularly in term loans. The break-out of fixed and variable costs is very important information."

"We certainly could do a better job of analysis with this type of income statement. It would facilitate the preparation of cash flow projections and permit more sophisticated analysis of the reasons for profit fluctuations.

"Break-even analysis is a key factor in seasonal business and our loan officers try to calculate this when data is available."

"Contribution margin reporting would greatly assist us in substantiating management's profit and cash flow forecasts. We use this type of data now, but it is largely derived by preparing rough statements based on information obtained in conversations with customers."

"We could strongly support this. It would be very useful in forecasting. A lender goes through the same procedure as management and needs the same data. This would not only aid us to prepare profit break-even analysis but also to calculate the break-even point for cash flows. However, fixed costs should be identified, particularly financial charges such as interest and rent."

Reactions of Company Executives to Contribution Margin Reporting

As has been indicated, segment contribution margin schedules can be included as supplementary data in financial reports of diversified companies without affecting the presentation of consolidated income or inventories. Indeed, a consolidated income statement prepared on a contribution margin basis for a highly diversified company probably would be less meaningful than the traditional income reporting format since the operations of some divisions may not lend themselves to this form of income reporting. Even more important, the merging of diverse segment contribution margins into a single consolidated figure would have only limited usefulness as a basis for forecasting future income. This is reflected in the following statement by one corporate executive.

> "One of our major manufacturing subsidiaries uses direct costing. However, it isn't applicable in our oil production operations. In farming operations we use a contribution approach because the major problem is to produce the crop that will make the largest contribution to fixed costs. Cattle costs and feeding costs are mostly variable, but there is a fairly long operating cycle. Hence, each subsidiary within the company has its own accounting policies. The situations are so varied that it wouldn't be meaningful to put together a consolidated income statement on the contribution margin basis."

While segment contribution margin reporting avoids arbitrary allocation of joint costs, certain problems remain. The first and most important question is whether or not the disclosure of segment profit structures will be damaging to profit opportunities. The reactions of corporate executives to this question will be examined in the next chapter.

Another important question is whether or not the several categories of costs can be distinguished with sufficient clarity to warrant application of the contribution margin approach in external reporting. Doubt was expressed by some company executives, as noted below.

> "The contribution margin method wouldn't work because of inability to define fixed and variable cost components."

> "We do not prepare internal contribution margin statements, but we do think in incremental terms in making decisions. Work is done by special studies. I am not opposed to this form of reporting, but this would require a revolutionary change in our accounting system, in management thinking, and in mechanical data handling facilities. In chemical operations most labor is fixed and there tends to be little cost really variable with output, in its influence on costs." (Note: other chemical companies use contribution margin reporting.)

"Management cannot justify its separation of costs into fixed and variable categories and shouldn't be placed in a position, under pressure, to do so."

"We couldn't break out fixed and variable costs in our business for our own information. Hence, the proposal to include contribution margin statements for stockholders can be dismissed as impractical." (Note: a leading competitor of this company does use contribution margin reporting internally.)

"In cement operations, short-run cost variations are non-linear."

Examination of the above comments shows that most reflect impressions traceable to direct costing and other applications of contribution margin analysis for internal decision-making purposes. As explained earlier in this chapter, these decisions usually are concerned with small segments and short time periods. On the other hand, segment operating reports which might be prepared for investors and creditors are likely to be for comparatively large segments and to cover annual periods. The nature and content of cost categories relevant for measuring *annual contribution to consolidated profit made by a large segment* is quite different from cost categories relevant to evaluating a single sales order or an individual item in a product line. The existing literature has given little attention to this subject.[3]

However, it must be recognized that these classifications will not be significant in reporting results from some types of business activities. As stated earlier, highly integrated operations with little separable cost cannot be divided into segments which are likely to be useful to analysts. Variability of costs with volume of sales will not be useful information for a segment in which annual sales volume is not an important variable affecting profits. An example is found where long-term contracts constitute the bulk of the work performed. Hence the form of segment reporting needs to be adapted to the operations carried on in each case.

Not all company executives expressed opposition to contribution margin reporting. Although a distinct minority, some agreed that analysts have a valid need for this information and stated that the information can be provided. Three statements illustrate this viewpoint:

---

[3] Mechanical techniques such as scatter charts and scanning of the chart of accounts have been stressed in the literature for distinguishing fixed and variable costs. Too often, there appears to be little realization of the fact that the content of these cost classifications can be specified only in relation to intended uses for the resulting information, and that content of classifications shifts with changes in the intended uses. Much confusion, in both literature and practice, is attributable to lack of clear conceptual thinking as a guide to application of contribution margin techniques.

"This company uses contribution margin reporting in all commercial divisions. It is the only way to understand what is going on because it is possible to relate activity to results. This can't be done any other way. However, we don't use contribution margin reporting for government business because pricing is not done that way. Our general books are on a full absorption cost basis. A fixed cost inventory component is carried in the general books and adjusted monthly on an overall basis. In regard to our commercial business I would like to see our general books and external reports on a direct cost basis. I believe they would be far more meaningful."

"This company uses direct costing but doesn't present its external income statement in contribution margin form. However, analysts know that we exclude fixed manufacturing costs from inventories and depreciation and depletion are stated separately. This, together with other information extracted in his plant visitations, should permit the analyst to make an estimate of our contribution margin."

"This company uses direct costing for internal purposes. The manner in which we itemize our costs in our income statements with the separation of certain other major items, gives the analyst an opportunity to prepare a break-even chart for the company (not diversified). I have seen such break-even charts and they are good tools for predicting the effect of volume changes on profit. While this method of reporting does aid the analyst in making forecasts, it wasn't deliberately devised for that purpose. Nevertheless, I can see no disadvantages flowing from contribution margin reporting externally. If the professional analyst understands our company better as a consequence of this type of reporting, the company benefits."

CHAPTER 4

Current Disclosure Practice

SUMMARY

Reporting for segments of a business is viewed by security analysts and bankers as an essential aspect of disclosure of information needed for making investment and credit decisions.

A distinct majority of the companies participating in this study now disclose sales for certain major segments or plan to do so. While 10 of the 70 companies included in the study also disclose product line margins, the 10 companies were chosen because they are among the very few in the United States which report segment profits.

Two different practices can be distinguished in reporting segment profit margins. In one group are companies which allocate all revenues and expenses to arrive at a net profit for each segment. In the other group are companies which report direct segment margins and do not allocate certain central corporate items of income and expense. Procedures followed by a number of companies are described in the chapter.

41

IN CURRENT LITERATURE, there is a common tendency to compartmentalize the issue of segment reporting. Yet, security analysts and bankers interviewed clearly identify segment reporting as one aspect of the much broader problem of adequate disclosure that directly relates to the segment reporting controversy.

DEMANDS FOR EXPENSE DISCLOSURE

Virtually without exception, security analysts and bankers complained about the failure of companies to itemize on their income statements major elements of cost of sales and selling and administrative expenses. Expense disclosure is inseparably linked to the problem of reporting for corporate segments. In order to make income projections, it is not sufficient for the analyst to be furnished with segment profits. He must also have sufficient detail to enable him to project the effect of expected changes which he learns about from discussions with company officials and other sources. Using advertising as an example, one analyst commented as follows:

> "We are not interested in comparing one company's advertising expenditures with another. Rather, we are concerned with trends. This leads to questions, such as: Is advertising defensive? Does it reflect newly introduced products, and if so, what are their potentials? What is the probable effect on share of the market profits?"

Although most corporate executives are strongly opposed to releasing these data, it seems likely that the pressure for such information will rise in the near future.

Expense Detail Reported

Among the 70 companies studied, the predominant income reporting practice is to present cost of sales (exclusive of depreciation) as a single figure, with depreciation and interest expense shown separately. However, as shown on page 43, some companies disclose additional operating details, although often this information is in other sections of the annual report rather than in the income statement.

Two of the most comprehensive and detailed examples of expense disclosure found among companies included in our study appear in Exhibit III. Although these two companies reveal their operating costs in greater detail than most companies, from the standpoint of the professional analyst even this disclosure is not entirely adequate.

Security analysts stress the need for supporting details on tax

Disclosure of Expense Details

Expenses Disclosed (Other than Depreciation and interest)	Number of Companies	Percent of Total Companies
Employment costs (salaries, wages, fringe benefits)	39	55.7%
Research and development	31	44.3
Pension costs	24	34.3
Materials, supplies and services	14	20.0
Taxes other than income	15	7.1
Freight and delivery	4	5.7
Sales promotion	1	.1
Advertising	1	.1
Freight and delivery	1	.1

Disclosure of Segment Sales

	Number of Companies	Percent of Total
Companies reporting sales breakdown by product lines and markets	7	10.4
Companies reporting sales breakdown by product lines only	37	55.2
Companies reporting sales breakdown by market only	5	7.5
Companies planning to provide sales breakdown in near future	5	7.5
Companies not prepared to include sales breakdown in annual report	13	19.4
	67	100%

EXHIBIT III

Examples of Expense Disclosure

Our Costs And Expenses Were:	1966	1965
Raw materials, supplies, fuel, advertising, etc., purchased from others	$505,524,000	$467,911,000
Wages, salaries, social security taxes and welfare benefits of employees	202,485,000	180,811,000
Salaries, social security taxes and welfare benefits of executives	1,852,000	1,828,000
Taxes imposed by federal, state and foreign governments (excluding social security taxes)	96,880,000	89,796,000
Depreciation—provision for wear and aging of facilities	13,745,000	12,738,000
Interest on money borrowed from others	1,879,000	2,125,000
Minority interests in net income of consolidated subsidiaries	2,844,000	2,232,000
Our Costs and Expenses Totaled.....	$825,209,000	$757,441,000

From American Home Products, 1966 Annual Report, *Operating Summary*.

Costs and expenses (Note I):	1966	1965
Employment costs:		
Wages and salaries	$317,041,000	$305,110,000
Employee benefits	60,291,000	56,758,000
	377,332,000	361,868,000
Materials, supplies, freight and other services	443,879,000	460,037,000
Depreciation and depletion	63,934,000	72,611,000
Interest and long-term debt expense	9,855,000	5,942,000
State, local and miscellaneous taxes	19,973,000	17,517,000
Federal income taxes, less investment tax credit of $4,543,000 in 1966 and $3,360,000 in 1965	39,051,000	28,314,000
	$954,024,000	$946,289,000

Note I—Costs and Expenses:

Cost of sales and operating expenses of $773,141,000 and selling, administrative and general expenses of $48,070,000 are included in the consolidated statement of income as "Employment costs" and "Materials, supplies, freight and other services." Repair and maintenance expenses included in these categories amounted to $117,272,000.

From Jones & Laughlin Steel Corp., 1966 Annual Report, *Consolidated Statement of Income*.

44

expenses. Owing to the magnitude and degree of variability in tax expenses, the analyst considers it imperative to have a breakdown of these costs when he projects future income. Yet, among the companies studied approximately 60% either combined all taxes or reported income tax separately without revealing the amounts incurred for other major taxes.

Analysts would like to see all companies provide tax details in the manner shown below.

	1966	1965
U. S. Federal and state gasoline and oil excise taxes (recovery thereof included in revenues from sales and services)	(000 omitted)	
	$145,443	$140,486
Income taxes:		
U. S.—Federal*	24,670	6,865
U. S.—state	1,130	1,317
Foreign**	63,200	37,718
	89,000	45,900
Operating taxes:		
Import duties and excise taxes— foreign	105,127	83,259
Ad valorem taxes	16,681	14,941
Production taxes	8,644	7,567
Unemployment and old age benefits taxes	6,231	4,170
Other taxes	5,382	4,503
	142,065	114,440
	$376,508	$300,826

*Reduced by $6,722,000 and $217,000 as a result of the allowable investment tax credit in 1966 and 1965, respectively.

**The 1965 provision reflects a reduction of $5,700,000 resulting from the remaining Libyan tax credit carry-forwards from 1964.

From Consolidated Oil Company, 1966 Annual Report, *Notes to Financial Statements.*

Other Income

"Other income" often represents a significant portion of net income and omission of its component elements complicates the efforts of the analyst to predict future income trends. However, among the 70 companies studied, approximately 55% report other income as a single figure. Two exceptions are shown on page 46.

| | Years Ended December 31 | |
	1965	1964
Transportation revenue	$ 1,048,965	$ 999,232
Interest and dividend income	4,536,926	3,890,809
Profit on foreign exchange	10,097,797	10,194,864
Profit on sales of stock in Longview Fibre Company	2,589,198	—
Other Items	585,193	106,601
Total	$18,858,079	$15,191,506

From International Paper Co., 1965 Annual Report,
Summary of Other Income—Net.

	1965	1964
EARNINGS FROM OPERATIONS	$ 566,595	$ 432,813
Interest Income	15,521	13,423
Dividends from subsidiary companies outside the U.S.	16,719	14,058
Royalties from subsidiary companies outside the U.S.	8,919	8,056
Other Income	8,425	5,275
EARNINGS BEFORE INCOME TAXES	$ 616,179	$ 473,625
Provision for United States, foreign and other Income taxes	298,000	226,000
NET EARNINGS	$ 318,179	$ 247,625

From Eastman Kodak Co., 1966 Annual Report,
Statement of Earnings.

Operating Statistics

Apart from the financial statements, many companies include additional operating statistics in their annual reports. This information often is very useful to security analysts in their efforts to appraise the future potential of a company. They would like to see these data expanded and more frequently included in annual reports. This particularly includes information relating to capital expenditures, order backlogs, price trends, share of the market, and unit production and sales where relevant.

CURRENT SEGMENT REPORTING PRACTICES
Disclosure of Segment Sales

The needs for segment information put forth by analysts have been described in earlier chapters. In regard to sales among the 70 companies (excluding three which are essentially single industry firms), approximately 80% presently include a breakdown of sales or are prepared to do so shortly. A summary of present practice and intent in disclosing segment sales is presented on page 43. When it is considered that outside the United States few companies even report sales, this appears to attest to the extent to which American management has recognized its responsibility to its stockholders. Although the SEC requires a sales breakdown in Form 10-K, there is no compulsion for companies to include this in annual reports.

Sales Reporting Requested by Analysts

In the current controversy on segment reporting, the question frequently has been raised as to what sales breakdowns are needed. Analysts would like to see sales data reported not only for product groups, but also by major markets, foreign versus domestic, and government (particularly defense) versus private customers. All of these are useful in terms of the analysts' income forecasting function.

Product line profit reports provide profitability ratios, as a percentage of sales, which can be ued in short term income projections. Sales segregated by major markets furnish a basis for forecasting future sales trends. Examples of product line and market sales disclosure appear in Exhibit IV. In some industries, where the data is amenable to such presentation (e.g., automobile, steel, aluminum, copper, lumber, cement, mining) analysts strongly prefer to have unit sales reported. Exhibits V and VI are examples of this type of sales reporting.

The importance of adequate sales disclosure is attested to by the fact that virtually every analyst's research report contains an extensive discussion and analysis of sales. The following are typical examples.

"——, like ——, is closely allied to the construction industry, in that it manufactures equipment to move men and materials. Approximately 70% of this division's volume is derived from the construction industry, with the balance going to the rail transportation industry. It is believed that sales to the rail industry will increase at a rate greater than sales to the construction field. —— is a major supplier of equipment to load and unload automobiles from highway trailers. The division's high price

—— crane has not been marketed successfully, since it is too heavy. It is currently being redesigned. Lower-priced models have met with satisfactory success. While this division has experienced some difficulties, sales and earnings should be well ahead of last year's level."

"Toiletries:—The marketing scramble over stainless steel blades obscured the company's rapid move to first place in the deodorant market with its ——, and aerosol spray. In fact, the company's brand toiletries' volume spurted from $15 million in 1963 to $30 million in 1964. A recently completed survey indicates that aerosol is based upon convenience and quality rather than price. While the study projected market growth at 11% per year through 1966, it also indicated that due to the acceleration of the market in recent months these figures were probably on the low side."

"Looking ahead, the company should continue to maintain its current 15% share of the total U.S. polyethylene market. In view of its present surplus domestic ethylene capacity the company should find an adequate and reasonably priced supplementary ethylene supply available for many years to come. The company's research and development will continue to provide new and improved resins. Based on general industry forecasts, the company's share of polyethylene output could exceed the 300 million lb. level by 1965. Assuming an average price of $.30 per lb. for all grades, 196X sales could approach the $100 million level. Profit margins may be expected to improve moderately from the present depressed level, for future increased production and continued process improvements and economies should more than offset possible future price reductions."

A segregation of sales between government and private sectors also is important to analysts because it permits them to give effect to the possibility of reorders or contract terminations. For a company heavily engaged in defense activities, this is a significant factor. Thus General Dynamics in its 1966 annual report states "Deliveries to government services and agencies represent 78 per cent of total sales in 1966." The two quotations from security analysts' reports which follow indicate how this information is used.

"Sales of the Atomic, Defense and Space group increased about 44% between 1958 and 1963. Profitability has generally been comparable to that of the defense industry in general except for 1961 when the company terminated its jet engine production. The company has been the primary supplier of nuclear reactor plants for submarines. In addition, the company is working on the design and development of the —— rocket motor, powered by nuclear fission. This engine may be used to propel craft in deep space missions after their initial escape from earth's gravity. Another contributor to the company's sales in this area is the production of missile launching and handling equipment for ——. The company has been a major producer of airborne and surface radar systems. . . ."

"While management does not give a divisional sales breakdown it is believed that this division accounts for some 50% of the company's volume and 80% of the current backlog of $35 million. . . . Sizeable

(Continued on page 55)

48

EXHIBIT IV
Disclosure of Sales by Product Lines and Markets

SALES BY PRODUCT LINE(1)
(Dollars in thousands)

	1957	1958	1959	1960	1961	1962	1963	1964	1965	1966
Subscription books	$25,164	$26,232	$31,520	$37,535	$34,894	$42,616	$41,175	$44,010	$46,005	$46,400
Home study					4,987	9,489	12,670	15,965	22,501	26,087
Publishing Textbooks:										
School				8,256	10,377	10,617	13,317	13,193	13,223	19,150
College(2)				6,815	8,287	10,095	11,962	13,730	16,494	18,253
Total				15,071	18,664	20,712	25,279	26,923	29,717	37,403
General books(3)				4,841	5,518	8,651	11,139	8,752	10,254	13,210
Total publishing				19,912	24,182	29,363	36,418	36,675	39,971	50,613
Supplementary and professional materials						807	1,276	1,586	1,987	2,456
Bookstores						4,058	4,296	4,850	5,660	6,951
Book clubs						3,111	3,708	4,195	4,776	5,105
Broadcasting	1,142	1,452	2,470	3,539	3,305	3,588	4,385	4,794	3,482	561
Special mail order— miscellaneous books and merchandise	305	289	520	2,528	3,323	2,946	569	1,053	1,847	3,207
Language instruction										6,922
Other	868	912	981	854	518	694	664	680	698	601
Total	$27,479	$28,885	$35,491	$64,368	$71,209	$96,672	$105,161	$112,808	$127,287	$148,903

(1) *Certain of these product line figures may vary from those in the text which are computed on an operating division basis. Sales in this table are historical rather than pro forma. Sales of Macmillan and other subsidiaries are not included for years prior to their acquisition by the Company.*

(2) *Includes professional, scientific and technical books.*

(3) *Includes paperbound books.*

From Crowell-Collier and Macmillan, Inc., 1966 Annual Report.

EXHIBIT IV (Continued)

SALES BY MARKET AREAS AND INDUSTRIES

Following is a breakdown of Hooker's principal market areas and the percentage contributions each made to the company's total sales of $284,095,000 during 1966:

- Plastics . . . 27%
- Farm Chemicals . . . 20%
- Chemical Intermediates . . . 15%
- Pulp & Paper Chemicals . . . 11%
- Metal Treating Chemicals . . . 11%
- International . . . 8%
- Detergent & Dry Cleaning Chemicals . . . 8%

The accompanying chart provides a review of the major industries which Hooker serves in these marketing areas and the approximate percentage of sales to each industry.

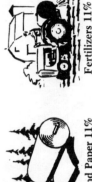

Pulp and Paper 11%

Fertilizers 11%

Metals & Metal Finishing 5%

Pesticides 5%

Animal Feed Additives 4%

Textiles & Synthetic Fibers 2%

Pharmaceuticals 2%

Glass 1%

International & Export 8%

Building 3%

Machinery 1%

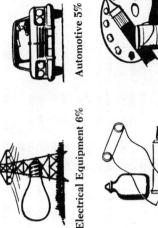

Soap & Detergents 7%

Fabricated Metal Products 3%

Food & Tobacco 1%

Fabricated Plastics Products 6%

Petroleum Products & Additives 3%

Rubber 1%

Electrical Equipment 6%

Plastic Materials 3%

Leather ½%

Automotive 5%

Dyes & Colors 2%

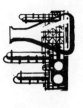

All Others 9½%

From Hooker Chemical Company, 1966 Annual Report.

EXHIBIT V

Illustration of Unit Sales Reporting

10-year summary of vehicle factory sales

Ford Motor Company and consolidated subsidiaries

U.S. and Canada—cars and trucks*

Cars	1966	1965	1964	1963	1962	1961	1960	1959	1958	1957
Ford U.S.										
Ford	960,905	1,044,066	878,353	909,886	721,848	711,847	916,073	1,352,110	985,166	1,506,469
Fairlane	295,419	251,222	233,177	318,291	385,138	58,795	—	—	—	—
Falcon	169,558	204,803	279,627	341,261	380,530	485,302	505,137	99,304	—	—
Mustang	566,367	564,999	293,807	—	—	—	—	—	—	—
Thunderbird	70,339	74,102	89,045	65,643	74,496	86,463	85,337	74,475	52,401	15,532
Mercury	152,220	189,967	125,482	118,577	108,454	109,394	160,049	156,253	129,088	274,521
Mercury Comet	127,195	161,982	194,568	149,683	145,018	185,419	196,876	—	—	—
Mercury Cougar	42,356	—	—	—	—	—	—	—	—	—
Lincoln Continental	51,374	43,921	37,231	32,858	32,962	32,538	19,998	29,248	26,319	36,336
Total**	2,435,733	2,535,062	2,131,747	1,959,579	1,929,100	1,685,015	1,884,023	1,741,855	1,221,909	1,883,045
Ford of Canada	181,426	184,169	161,688	142,887	120,967	99,679	95,855	101,669	92,135	110,472
Cars, total	2,617,159	2,719,231	2,293,435	2,102,466	2,050,067	1,784,694	1,979,878	1,843,524	1,314,044	1,993,517
Industry	9,288,835	10,009,712	8,308,462	8,167,464	7,363,164	5,868,179	7,000,217	5,891,219	4,555,648	6,452,953
Percent of industry	28.2	27.2	27.6	25.7	27.8	30.4	28.3	31.3	28.8	30.9
Trucks*										
Ford U.S.	568,129	543,339	448,431	425,527	372,893	335,654	338,311	347,042	242,703	338,728
Ford of Canada	54,021	40,795	37,414	32,906	25,747	19,902	19,883	18,587	17,539	24,652
Trucks, total***	622,150	584,134	485,845	458,433	398,640	355,556	358,194	365,629	260,242	363,380
Industry	1,926,533	1,893,721	1,650,372	1,560,761	1,321,089	1,197,387	1,263,490	1,205,539	939,098	1,177,965
Percent of industry	32.3	30.8	29.4	29.4	30.2	29.7	28.3	30.3	27.7	30.8
Cars and trucks, total	3,239,309	3,303,365	2,779,280	2,560,899	2,448,707	2,140,250	2,338,072	2,209,153	1,574,286	2,356,897
Industry	11,215,368	11,903,433	9,958,834	9,728,225	8,684,253	7,065,566	8,263,707	7,096,758	5,494,746	7,630,918
Percent of industry	28.9	27.8	27.9	26.3	28.2	30.3	28.3	31.1	28.7	30.9

Outside U.S. and Canada—cars and trucks

Cars										
Britain	441,128	501,653	517,167	492,361	357,561	341,057	383,392	321,399	292,019	240,401
Germany	441,950	464,279	355,573	348,982	269,548	230,352	181,771	133,055	109,017	69,248
Australia	50,135	40,311	36,214	36,705	45,029	26,572	14,361	—	—	—
Argentina	16,198	15,442	11,966	2,043	—	—	—	—	—	—
Mexico	17,743	7,842	—	—	—	—	—	—	—	—
Cars, total	967,154	1,029,527	920,920	880,091	672,138	597,981	579,524	454,454	401,036	309,649
Trucks										
Britain	110,982	84,676	91,121	83,542	87,909	92,568	91,327	85,367	69,948	52,618
Germany	45,630	32,346	38,479	36,096	35,831	31,682	27,552	21,858	16,831	20,799
Brazil	13,783	11,905	11,842	12,819	21,622	14,044	19,037	—	—	—
Australia	7,009	7,656	7,051	7,603	7,746	4,328	—	—	—	—
Argentina	13,536	13,233	9,862	—	—	—	—	—	—	—
Mexico	9,379	4,624	—	—	—	—	—	—	—	—
Trucks, total	200,319	154,440	158,355	140,060	153,108	142,622	137,916	107,225	86,779	73,417
Cars and trucks, total	1,167,473	1,183,967	1,079,275	1,020,151	825,246	740,603	717,440	561,679	487,815	383,066
Worldwide tractors										
Ford U.S.	38,620	31,047	25,880	26,046	27,489	24,319	26,806	45,014	45,685	44,874
Overseas	79,768	76,978	68,292	85,198	74,696	71,962	71,474	65,817	59,375	45,127
Tractors, total	118,388	108,025	94,172	111,244	102,185	96,281	98,280	110,831	105,060	90,001
Total worldwide factory sales	4,525,170	4,595,357	3,952,727	3,692,294	3,376,138	2,977,134	3,153,792	2,881,663	2,167,161	2,829,964

*Factory sales are by source of manufacture, except that Ford U.S. exports to Canada are included as factory sales of Ford of Canada and Ford of Canada exports to the United States are included as factory sales of Ford U.S.

**Includes an aggregate of 229,888 units of car lines no longer produced by the Company.

***Includes buses.

Source of Industry Data: Automobile Manufacturers Association.

From Ford Motor Company, 1966 Annual Report.

EXHIBIT VI

Illustration of Unit Sales Reporting

The table below shows J&L's production of coke, iron, and raw steel for 1966 compared with the prior year.

	Net Tons	
	1966	1965
Coke	3,648,000	3,641,000
Iron	5,484,000	5,583,000
Raw steel	7,726,000	7,280,000

Shipments and Distribution

Shipments of 5,341,000 tons in 1966 established a J&L all-time record and an increased share of the steel industry's total shipments.

During the year adjustments were made in the prices for certain of the products we sell. Some of these adjustments were upward and some adjustments were downward. However, the net effect was a modest increase in average prices.

As shown below, there was little change in the mix of products shipped in 1966, as compared with 1965.

	1966	1965
Hot and cold rolled and coated sheets and strip	46%	47%
Tubular products	13	13
Hot rolled and cold finished bars	14	13
Plates and structural shapes	10	10
Tin plate and black plate	8	9
Wire products	3	3
All other	6	5
	100%	100%

EXHIBIT VI (Continued)

The following table also indicates little change in market distribution compared to 1965.

	1966	1965
Automotive	28%	30%
Jobbers and dealers	17	18
Containers	9	10
Machinery and equipment	9	8
Construction	8	8
Household appliances and office equipment	7	6
Oil and gas	5	5
All other domestic consumers	16	14
Export	1	1
	100%	100%

Looking ahead, the additional steel which will result from J&L's current expansion program will present a commercial challenge to our sales force and an opportunity to serve customers from another production location. A nearby source of steel is increasingly of interest to steel users. We have increased J&L's sales effort through additions to the sales force in those new marketing areas which we will serve.

From Jones & Laughlin Steel Corp., 1966 Annual Report.

Sales Reporting Requested by Analysts
(Continued from page 47)

> new orders are expected to be awarded before the year end. Although the war in Viet Nam has aided the volume in this division commercial and normal defense business should offset any down-turn in Viet Nam. . . . The company is also an important supplier to the Navy's nuclear submarine program. This operation is expected to continue to expand over the next several years. . . ."

A breakout of foreign sales, where material, enables the analyst to assess the growth potential and risk involved in particular countries or world areas. Accordingly, in most cases a segregation of sales by geographical areas, rather than product lines, is sufficient for foreign sales. Examples of such disclosure are presented in Exhibit VII. The importance of isolating foreign sales is emphasized in the following statement which appeared in *Barrons* on November 13, 1967. It will be noted that five days later devaluation of the pound sterling actually took place.

EXHIBIT VII

Disclosure of Foreign Sales

Kodak companies operating outside the United States had another good year, as sales and earnings moved to new highs again in 1966.

	1966	1965	*Increase*
Sales (in millions)	$582.7	$495.7	18%
Net Earnings (in millions)	$ 49.1	$ 43.0	14%
Percent of Sales	8.4%	8.7%	

The companies abroad experienced continued growth in demand for their products and services; almost all product groups sold at higher volume levels. Of the three territories, Canada and Latin America had the best percentage gain, as sales rose to $109.6 million, 21 percent higher than in 1965. Close behind were the companies operating in the British Isles and Continental Europe, with an increase of 18 percent, to $420.3 million. This comparison is, of course, affected by the addition of the new subsidiary companies in Sweden and Finland during 1966. Also, a new company, Ectona Fibres Limited, was formed in England to manufacture cellulose acetate cigarette filter material; this company is 60 percent owned. The Africa, Asia, Australasia and Far East group, despite political unrest and depressed economic conditions in some areas, still moved 6 percent ahead of last year, to $63.7 million.

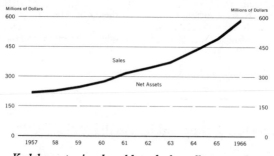

Kodak companies abroad have had excellent growth

From Eastman Kodak Company, 1966 Annual Report.

U.S. sales accounted for 48.7 per cent of the total in 1966, increasing at a faster rate than foreign sales. Sales by major geographical areas were as follows:

	1966	1965	*Change*
	(*Amounts in Millions*)		
United States	$ 510.7	$470.3	+ 8.6%
Europe	284.4	237.1	+ 4.8
Latin America	124.4	110.6	+12.5
Far East	82.9	87.5	− 5.3
Africa and the Near East	50.1	46.1	+ 8.7
Canada	32.7	28.2	+16.0
Total	$1,049.2	$979.8	+ 7.1%

From The Singer Company, 1966 Annual Report.

"In all, the Canadian, German and Mexican operations contributed 24% of last year's per share earnings, and domestic stores (including Puerto Rico), 43%. The remainder came from the British subsidiary. If anything, Woolworth Ltd. of England's share is likely to shrink again this year, with most of the gains coming from the U.S. and the other foreign activities.

"Over in England, the U.K. company is adding about nine outlets, including one Woolco unit to its roster of 1,130 stores; nevertheless, as indicated most of the gains are coming from the U.S. and other foreign activities.

"The major threat over there, of course, is the much talked about possibility of devaluation of the pound. Any write down that would result from such a move probably would be reflected in the income statement as an extraordinary item, rather than charged against surplus. . . ."[1]

Disclosure of Product Line Profits

Of the 68 companies participating in the study which produce more than one group of products, 10 presently are reporting profits by major product lines. However, these companies were included in the survey for this very reason. When it is considered that only some two dozen major concerns in the United States report product line profits today, these 10 companies represent a significant portion of the total. A brief description of the reporting procedures used by these companies follows:

Martin Marietta
Sales and earnings are reported for two major product groups: aerospace and commercial. The latter category is further subdivided into cement and lime, chemicals, and rock products. To these profits are added the company's 61% interest in the earnings of an unconsolidated subsidiary (Bunker-Ramo Corporation). All corporate revenues and expenses are allocated to product groups.

Kaiser Industries
The operating profit of divisions representing product groups and 100% owned consolidated subsidiaries is reported with no allocation of corporate expenses and revenues. To this is added the company's interest in the earnings of three affiliated companies (per cent ownership, 78.8%, 41.4%, and 39.4%).

Kern County Land Company
The contribution to consolidated earnings is divided into three broad categories: oil and minerals, manufacturing, and land-use operations. Each of these categories is further subdivided. For example, land-use operations are segregated into agriculture, water, cattle, real estate, and miscellaneous. No corporate revenues and expenses (except for income taxes) are allocated to these segments.

Olin Mathieson
Income is reported for five product groups: chemicals, metals, Winchester-Western, forest products, and Squibb. All corporate revenue and

[1] *Barrons,* November 13, 1967, p. 9.

expenses, exclusive of interest on debt, are allocated to the product groups.

National Distillers and Chemical Corp.

Sales and operating profits are reported for five divisions: liquor, chemicals, metals, international, and H. W. Loud Company. Corporate revenue and expenses are not allocated to divisions.

Wallace and Tiernan

Sales and net income are reported for three product lines: pharmaceuticals, chemicals and equipment. All corporate revenues and expenses are distributed to these product groups.

Textron

Sales and income are reported for four product lines: aerospace, consumer, industrial and metal products. All corporate expenses and revenues, except income tax, are assigned to product lines.

Singer

Sales and net income are reported under three marketing categories, viz., products for the home, industry, and business. All corporate revenues and expenses are allocated. A further sales breakdown is provided by product lines for each of these major categories. For example, sales of products for the home are reported under the following categories: sewing machines, major appliances, home entertainment and equipment, and other. Income is not reported for these product lines.

Southern Pacific

A statistical supplement to the annual report is published which contains balance sheet and income data for 26 consolidated subsidiaries. Since these are separate legal entities, parent company expenses are not allocated. In effect, apart from other significant statistical data included, this supplement presents a consolidating statement, a form of reporting considered highly informative by bankers and security analysts.

Transamerica

This is essentially a holding company. Like Southern Pacific, a statistical supplement is published which includes a statement of net earnings contributed by each major source, i.e., life insurance companies, finance and leasing companies, property and casualty insurance companies, real estate and title insurance companies, and manufacturing companies. The contribution of each major subsidiary in each of these groups is also reported. In addition, consolidated income statements and balance sheets are presented for each of these groups.

Allocation Procedures

Different procedures are used by these companies in assigning corporate revenues and expenses to product groups. Wallace and Tiernan and Singer allocate all such items to product lines, whereas National Distillers and Chemical Corporation makes no such allocations. Martin Marietta distributes all corporate revenues and expenses to its segments except its share in the earnings of a major unconsolidated subsidiary (Bunker-Ramo). Olin Mathieson allocates all net corporate expenses except income taxes to its product lines. On the other hand, Kern County Land Company allocates only income taxes to its segments.

In discussions with company executives, the NAA research team gained the impression that in the aggregate, net corporate expenses generally represent about 1-2% of sales. This might seem to confirm any margin of error resulting from the allocation procedure to tolerable limits. However, statistics of this type may be deceiving. In some companies, particularly those which are highly centralized and research oriented, corporate expenses tend to be proportionably greater than in other companies. The magnitude of these expenses also depends to a considerable extent on how corporations classify particular items. Moreover, certain corporate revenues and expenses may fluctuate sharply from period to period, especially such items as abnormal gains or losses and income from unconsolidated subsidiaries and affiliates.

Even if net corporate expenses were in the range of 1-2% of sales, they generally would constitute a significant portion of net income and thus have a material effect on reported earnings of product lines. For example, in the case of National Distillers and Chemical Corporation, net corporate expenses amounted to 1.5% of sales in 1966 and 1.3% in 1965. However, as a percent of income, these expenses were 34.2% and 30.4% respectively for the two years.

Different allocation procedures are used to assign corporate revenues and expenses to product groups. This is reflected in the following statements made by vice presidents of two of the companies presently reporting product line profits.

"In this company, central corporate costs total about $1.4 millions a year or about 1.5% of sales and 15% of net income. Of this amount, about one-third is assigned to divisions as direct charges as follows:

1. Research and development costs are accumulated by projects and those projects undertaken for the benefit of specific products or processes are charged directly to the division benefited.
2. Legal costs are charged to divisions on the basis of time spent on work done for each division.
3. The annual audit fee is broken down according to the time spent by the auditors with each division's accounts.
4. Tax work done for individual divisions is charged directly.

Charges for these costs are billed to divisions monthly. Budgeted rates are used for computing charges to avoid fluctuations for which divisions are not responsible.

"The remaining two thirds of central office costs are common to the divisions. These are arbitrarily allocated to divisions on the ratio of division pre-tax budgeted net profit to total budgeted pre-tax profit for the company. The only justification for this basis is the ability of divisions to pay. Allocations of central corporate costs make divisions aware that these costs must be recovered in pricing products. There has been little objection from division management; they are responsible only for controllable costs before these allocations.

59

EXHIBIT VIII
Disclosure of Product Line Profits

	SALES			EARNINGS		
	1966	1965	Change	1966	1965	Change
	(In Thousands)			(In Thousands)		
Aerospace Group	$404,225	$355,868	13.6%	$ 9,428	$13,057	(27.8%)
Commercial Group						
Cement and Lime Division	113,900	111,215	2.4%	11,687	12,524	(6.7%)
Chemical Division	90,268	82,191	9.8%	8,627	7,337	17.6%
Rock Products Division	61,428	53,832	14.1%	6,552	5,437	20.5%
Total	$669,821	$603,106	11.1%	$36,294	$38,355	(5.4%)
Share of Profit (Loss) of						
The Bunker-Ramo Corporation				672	(7,841)	
Net Earnings				$36,966	$30,514	21.1%

From Martin Marietta, 1966 Annual Report.

DIVISIONAL OPERATING RESULTS

Divisions	Net Sales (000 omitted)			Operating Profit (000 omitted)		
	1966	1965	1964	1966	1965	1964
Liquor	$497,474	$469,828	$430,471	$46,840	$45,763	$39,467
Chemicals	133,432	135,952	137,554	24,216	16,444	14,633
Metals	235,095	193,677	216,962	19,933	10,486	5,923
International	11,696	10,924	9,841	2,553	966	28
H. W. Loud Co.	20,615	18,650	16,113	76	1,213	963
Totals	$898,312	$829,031	$810,941	$88,512	$70,514	$59,032

NOTE: Sales of 50 per cent owned domestic affiliates are not included in consolidated net sales; however, the Company's share of net earnings of these affiliates, including Reactive Metals, Inc.. is allocated to the Chemical Division.

From National Distillers and Chemical Corp. 1966 Annual Report.

EXHIBIT VIII (Continued)

Our net income from all operations in 1966 was $73,522,000. The following table shows what each business area contributed to this total after assuming a share of all undistributed corporate expenses (based on assets, sales and number of employees):

CHEMICALS 20%
METALS 18%
WINCHESTER-WESTERN 17%
FOREST PRODUCTS, FINE PAPER, & FILM 21%
SQUIBB 24%

From Olin Mathieson Corporation, 1966 Annual Report.

PHARMACEUTICAL DIVISIONS

Operating revenues increased by 8.6% from $25,869,000 in 1964 to $28,105,000 in 1965. Pharmaceutical net income was $2,917,000 in 1964 and $3,475,000 in 1965, an increase of 19.1%.

CHEMICAL DIVISIONS

Operating revenues were $37,188,000 in 1965 compared with $35,284,000 in 1964, an increase of 5.4% while net income rose by 5.1% from $3,413,000 in 1964 to $3,588,000 in 1965.

EQUIPMENT DIVISIONS

Operating revenues rose from $26,173,000 to $29,418,000, an increase of 12.4%. Net income more than doubled, rising from $1,078,000 to $2,228,000.

From Wallace & Tiernan Corporation, 1965 Annual Report.

PRODUCT GROUP	1966 SALES	1966 PRETAX INCOME	1966 PER CENT RETURN ON SALES (*Pretax*)
Aerospace	$463,037 41%	$17,088 20%	3.7%
Consumer	223,414 20%	21,916 26%	9.8%
Industrial	239,712 21%	18,244 22%	7.6%
Metal Product	206,011 18%	27,465 32%	13.3%
Total	$1,132,174 100%	$84,713 100%	7.5%

From Textron Corporation, 1966 Annual Report.

"This year one of our divisions has a low profit. This offered tempta-tions to alter the allocation basis to conceal the results from stockhold-ers. This company would not do this. We feel it is best to be frank with stockholders."

"Allocation problems are relatively minor in this company. There is little interdivision trading due to differences in products. Divisional or-ganization and product groups coincide. Policy, money, capital expendi-tures are controlled centrally. Operations are controlled by divisions. All research and development and most legal and accounting work is done in the divisions. Joint costs are home office costs and amount to approxi-mately .8% of sales and 14% of net income. The allocation basis used is the Massachusetts formula which gives weight to payroll, sales, inven-tory, receivables, and net property. This formula was chosen because it is acceptable for state tax purposes and to the Department of Defense for allocating costs in reimbursement contracts."

Martin Marietta has a 61% ownership interest in the Bunker-Ramo Corporation. This subsidiary is not consolidated but ac-counted for as an investment by the equity method. All other subsidiaries are consolidated. In 1965, Martin Marietta's share in the net loss of Bunker-Ramo amounted to $7,840,966 and in 1966 its interest in the profit of this subsidiary was $671,912. These amounts were reported separately on the income statement and not allocated to product groups. Had such allocations been made in 1965, reported group profits would have been approximately 20% lower. Clearly, the assignment of this loss to product lines in 1965 would have created erroneous impressions as to their profitability. Yet, other companies studied do make these allocations in cal-culating segment profits, although the amounts involved may not always be as material. Companies that maintain unconsolidated subsidiaries at cost rather than equity are faced with the same allocation problem in regard to dividends received.

It seems apparent that the allocation of corporate revenues and expenses to product groups involves considerable judgment and can result in distortions of reported segment profits. While dis-tribution of these items to divisions may be desirable for internal reasons, e.g., to assure total cost recovery in long-run pricing de-cisions, there would seem to be substantially less justification for making these allocations to product lines in external reporting. One possible reason for assigning these items to product lines is the fear that some report readers may be confused as to the dis-tinctions between segment profit and net income. National Dis-tillers and Chemical Corporation resolves this problem by reporting its total "divisional" operating profit as a separate line item on its consolidated income statement, as shown in Exhibit IX. Thus, its

EXHIBIT IX

Divisional Operating Profit Shown before Corporate Expenses

NATIONAL DISTILLERS AND CHEMICAL CORPORATION
and Subsidiary Companies

CONSOLIDATED STATEMENT OF INCOME

	1966	1965
Net sales	$898,312,000	$829,031,000
Cost of goods sold	742,168,000	692,013,000
Gross profit	156,144,000	137,018,000
Share of net earnings of 50% owned domestic affiliates	5,012,000	467,000
Selling, advertising and other divisional expenses	72,644,000	66,971,000
Divisional operating profit	88,512,000	70,514,000
Corporate and general expenses	6,424,000	6,783,000
Interest on long-term debt	8,045,000	7,370,000
Other income (net)	547,000	3,614,000
	74,590,000	59,975,000
Provision for taxes on income (Note 5)	33,910,000	28,690,000
Net income for the year	$ 40,680,000	$ 31,285,000
Net income per share of common stock	$3.09	$2.37

Note: It will be observed that this company credits "Share of net earnings of 50% owned domestic affiliates" to divisional operating profit. These earnings relate directly to the Chemical product group and require no allocation.

---

divisional or product line profitability statement (shown in Exhibit VIII) constitutes a supporting schedule to the consolidated statement of income.

While the method used by National Distillers and Chemical Corporation avoids allocation of joint corporate revenues and expenses, it does not take the additional step desired by analysts, which would be to provide detail of divisional operating costs, including a distinction between long-run fixed costs and other costs.

CHAPTER 5

External Reporting for
Legal Corporate Segments

SUMMARY

While consolidated reports are commonly used to present accounts of an enterprise as a whole, security analysts and bankers feel that such reports need to be supplemented by certain types of information about individual subsidiaries. Bankers are particularly interested in corporate ownership of assets which constitute security for loans. Hence, bankers generally ask for consolidating schedules or financial statements for the major subsidiaries. Security analysts are more concerned with disclosure of pertinent information on foreign subsidiaries.

Variations in practice prevalent in preparing consolidated reports were often cited by both groups of interviewees. Examples were given where the choice of consolidation method may affect the analyst's appraisal of income, growth, and risk.

Certain changes are suggested in the chapter with the purpose of improving usefulness of reporting for subsidiaries.

T HE PRECEDING SECTIONS of this study have been concerned with external reporting for business segments, such as divisions, product lines, and markets which are ordinarily not separate legal entities. However, corporate segments also may comprise legal entities whose voting stock is entirely or partially owned by the company in question. These relationships create special accounting and reporting problems.

When all of the stock of another company is acquired, its legal existence may be terminated and its assets merged with those of the acquiring company. When this occurs, the acquired company generally assumes divisional status. On the other hand, when a company owns all or a majority of the voting stock of another company, and the latter's separate legal existence is continued, a parent-subsidiary relationship exists. Accountants consider it desirable under such circumstances to prepare consolidated financial statements which combine the assets, liabilities, and operating results of these corporations. The important advantage of consolidated statements is that they eliminate intercompany transactions and in effect treat a group of legally separate but closely related companies as a single economic entity in conformance to the realities of the situation. However, under certain circumstances consolidated statements are not considered appropriate, as for example, when the operations of the companies are sufficiently different (e.g., where a manufacturer owns an insurance or finance company), in case of blocked currencies, or when the subsidiary is in the process of liquidation.

ATTITUDES OF SECURITY ANALYSTS AND BANKERS

Needs for Supplementary Information

The security analysts and bankers interviewed frequently expressed dissatisfaction with the variations in reporting practices and with what they consider to be inadequate disclosure of relevant information about consolidated subsidiaries.

Bankers were especially concerned about the failure of parent companies to report separately their assets and legal obligations. When loans are made to the parent, a bank does not have recourse to the merged assets of the group but only to those of the company with which it has contracted. Moreover, a knowledge of intercompany receivables and payables, which are eliminated in consolidation, may have an influence of the granting of credit. In long-term loans, bankers are interested in the extent to which profits of the dominant company are offset by losses of the subordinate companies and vice versa. For these reasons, bankers often stated a preference for consolidated statements or consolidated reports accompanied by individual income statements and balance sheets for major subsidiaries.

Security analysts expressed particular concern about disclosure of pertinent information on foreign subsidiaries. Since such investments often are maintained at cost, analysts would like to see the equity in the underlying assets disclosed as well as any material gain or loss on currency fluctuation and the amount of dividends included in consolidated income. They also feel that companies should disclose the sales and income earned in different countries or major world areas. This would provide them with a better basis for predicting the effect on a company's consolidated income of unstable regional conditions, monetary changes, or other peculiar circumstances in these foreign countries.

Variations in Consolidation Practices

Security analysts were critical of the latitude permitted companies in regard to the consolidation of subsidiaries. Failure to merge the assets, liabilities and revenue accounts of a subsidiary affects growth trends and other ratios compiled by analysts. Moreover, the acceptability of alternative methods of accounting for unconsolidated subsidiaries can have an important impact on consolidated income and it is not inconceivable that management's choice of method may be influenced by the result it wishes to show.

When a subsidiary is not consolidated, the parent company's investment may be accounted for under either the equity or cost methods, with varying results. If the cost method is used, the investment account is maintained at original cost and dividends received from the subsidiary are included in consolidated income. Under the equity method the parent company's investment account is increased or decreased periodically to reflect its proportionate share of changes in the net assets of the subsidiary since the date of acquisition. Dividends received are treated as a reduction in the investment account and excluded from income. An indication of the impact on income for these alternative methods can be adduced from the following cases. It should be noted that, in citing these examples, sufficient information was contained in annual reports of these companies to permit analysis. In the large majority of reports, such information was not included.

Eastman Kodak (1966 Annual Report): The company maintains its investment in subsidiaries outside the United States at cost (or lower) which amounted to $85,504,000 less reserves of $15,478,000. The company's equity in net assets of these subsidiaries was $329,487,000 and its equity in 1966 earnings was $48,793,000. Dividends from these subsidiaries included in consolidated income were $16,719,000. Assuming, as is generally the case, that had the company used the equity method it would not have deducted U.S. taxes on undistributed earnings of subsidiaries and that the tax rate applied to dividends received was 50%, consolidated income would have been approximately $40,434,000 or 12.7% greater under the equity method ($48,793,000 less .50 × $16,719,000).[1]

American Smelting and Refining Company (1966 Annual Report): This company has investments in unconsolidated subsidiaries which are accounted for at cost or less of $29,092,485 with market value of $253,590,600. Had the company used the equity method its consolidated income would have been $13,835,000 or approximately 20% higher (since no mention is made of dividends it is assumed that none were received).

Philip Morris (1966 Annual Report): Using the equity method, this company included $2,627,290 in consolidated income representing its equity in the earnings of unconsolidated subsidiaries. Assuming no U.S. taxes were applied or dividends received (this is not indicated in the report), consolidated earnings were 7.7% greater than they would have been under the cost method.

Kaiser Aluminum & Chemical (1966 Annual Report): During this year the company changed its method of accounting for investments in less than wholly owned foreign subsidiaries from cost to equity. As a consequence, consolidated income for the year was increased by $1,265,-000 or 2.2% of income before the change.

Fibreboard Paper Products Corporation (1965 Annual Report): This company used the equity method of accounting for its wholly owned Australian subsidiary. The cost of the investment in this subsidiary was $65,789 and is reflected on the balance sheet under the equity method at $777,591. The net difference has been included in consolidated net income. While we cannot tell precisely what the effect has been on income in any given year, it could have been significant (dependent on the life of the investment) since the average annual income of the company from 1961-1965 amounted to $13,548,000.

United Merchants (1966 Annual Report): This company consolidates its foreign subsidiaries. These companies contributed $7,995,984 to consolidated income. United States income taxes are not provided for on undistributed earnings. Assuming no dividends were received, income was approximately 33% greater than it would have been had the company not consolidated these subsidiaries and maintained the investment at cost.

Where the equity method is used, analysts prefer to have the amount of undistributed earnings included in consolidated income revealed together with sales and other relevant information. In gen-

---

[1] Under certain circumstances, dividends received from foreign corporations may be offset by the 85% dividend credit granted on dividends from taxable domestic corporations. On the probability that this is not the case here, the dividend credit is excluded from the calculations.

eral, analysts favored the cost method although their major complaint was with the lack of uniformity that exists in accounting for foreign subsidiaries. Thus, one security analyst commented:

> "This is a very troublesome area due largely to a lack of uniformity and inadequate disclosure. I believe that companies with foreign subsidiaries should reveal what part of their foreign profits is really available to them as a U.S. parent after allowance for U.S. and foreign taxes. I prefer to have only dividends received included in earnings with a footnote regarding total equity in undistributed earnings. I would also like to see all companies disclose the basis for converting foreign assets, liabilities and income together with any loss or gain on the conversion."

Variations in Consolidation Practices

Annual reports of the 70 companies studied revealed considerable variation in the basis used for consolidation and the method of accounting for unconsolidated subsidiaries. These differences are summarized below:

Basis for Consolidation

	Companies	Percent of Total
All majority owned domestic and foreign companies	15	21.4%
All significantly owned domestic and foreign companies	5	7.2
Only wholly owned domestic and foreign companies	11	15.7
Only wholly owned domestic (including Canadian) companies	7	10.0
Miscellaneous bases[2]	13	18.1
No information provided	19	27.6
	70	100.0%

Basis of Accounting for Unconsolidated Subsidiaries

	Companies	Percent of Total
Cost	21	63.6
Equity	12	36.4
	33	100.0

A substantial variation also was found in regard to the extent of disclosure of supporting details. For example, only one-third of the

---

[2] Additional variations in this category include "All domestic and *some* foreign companies," "All majority owned domestic and foreign companies *except* finance and real estate companies," etc.

companies using the cost method of accounting for unconsolidated subsidiaries indicated the underlying equity in the subsidiary's net assets. Only two companies among the 12 using the equity method disclosed the share of subsidiaries' net income included in consolidated income.

In regard to foreign subsidiaries, 18 companies provided no supporting details. Twenty-two companies reported separately the assets and liabilities of their foreign subsidiaries, 20 the income and 10 the sales. Only five companies stated the amount of dividends received and six the gain or loss on translation of foreign currency. Eight companies stated that no United States income tax was provided on undistributed earnings of foreign subsidiaries included in their consolidated income. One can only speculate whether other companies did or did not include this tax deduction, and the difference can be material.

SUGGESTIONS FOR IMPROVEMENT IN ACCOUNTING FOR SUBSIDIARIES

It is apparent that variations in accounting for subsidiaries can have a significant effect on reported earnings. This, together with lack of disclosure of data considered relevant to appraisal of securities for major subsidiaries is a matter of serious concern to professional analysts. Analysts are willing to concede that a particular subsidiary, the nature of its activities, and the environment within which it operates justify management discretion in the selection of an appropriate method of accounting provided disclosure is made of methods chosen. Yet interpretation of financial reports would be facilitated by narrowing differences in accounting practices. Where differences are not essential to reflect different circumstances certain possibilities are described below.[3]

(1) As has been indicated, there is considerable variation in company policies regarding the basis for consolidation. This continues despite the definition of what constitutes a controlling interest (i.e., over 50% of the voting stock) in AICPA Bulletin No. 5. An unambiguous reaffirmation of this statement together with clarification concerning the specific circumstances under which a subsidiary may be excluded from the consolidation should be helpful.

(2) A single method of accounting could prevail for unconsolidated subsidiaries. Only one of the companies participating in this study was observed to be following this practice. In its recent

---

[3] A research study by the AICPA on this topic is now in process.

Opinion No. 10 the Accounting Principles Board recommended the equity method in the following words:[4]

> "If, in consolidated financial statements, a domestic subsidiary is not consolidated, the Board's opinion is that unless circumstances are such as those referred to in paragraph 2 of ARB-No. 51, the investment in the subsidiary should be adjusted for the consolidated group's share of accumulated undistributed earnings and losses since acquisition. This practice is sometimes referred to as the "equity" method. In reporting periodic consolidated net income, the earnings or losses of the unconsolidated subsidiary (or group of subsidiaries) should generally be presented as a separate item. The amount of such earnings or losses should give effect to amortization, if appropriate, of any difference between the cost of the investment and the equity in net assets at date of acquisition and to any elimination of intercompany gains or losses that would have been made had the subsidiary been consolidated. If desired, dividends received by members of the consolidated group from the unconsolidated subsidiary may be shown parenthetically or by footnote (See also paragraph 21 of ARB 51 which relates to disclosure of assets and liabilities of unconsolidated subsidiaries)."

(3) The AICPA *Inventory of Generally Accepted Accounting Principles* appears to support exclusion of foreign subsidiaries from consolidated financial statements and the use of the cost method in accounting for them.[5]

> "4. A sound procedure for United States companies to follow is to show earnings from foreign operations in their own account only to the extent that funds have been received in the United States or unrestricted funds are available for transmission thereto. Appropriate provisions should be made also for known losses. . . .

> "8. In view of the uncertain values and availability of the assets and net income of foreign subsidiaries subject to controls and exchange restrictions and the consequent unrealistic statements of income that may result from the translation of many foreign currencies into dollars, careful consideration should be given to the fundamental question of whether it is proper to consolidate the statements of foreign subsidiaries with the statements of United States companies. Whether consolidation for foreign subsidiaries is decided upon or not, adequate disclosure for foreign operations should be made."

Among 70 companies studied, to the extent that the basis for consolidation was disclosed in their annual reports, the majority consolidate foreign subsidiaries. Other companies exclude foreign subsidiaries from their consolidated statements and account for their investments at cost, including only dividends received in consolidated earnings. The extent to which this practice reflects difficulties in making realistic translations of foreign currency net assets and nonconvertibility of currencies is unknown. It is possible that

---

[4] *Omnibus Opinion No. 10,* Opinions of the Accounting Principles Board of the AICPA, December 1966, pp. 142-143.
[5] Pp. 328-29.

some companies are simply highly conservative in accounting for investments in foreign subsidiaries. From the investor's point of view, consolidation would seem to provide information more useful for investment appraisal purposes except where foreign currencies are highly unstable and transfers of funds to the United States cannot be made. Less conservatism in accounting for foreign subsidiaries probably calls for freedom to establish reserves for possible losses, with the nature and amount of such reserves fully disclosed. This practice would allow management to express its uncertainty about the realization of foreign currency earnings without simply not reporting them.

(4) For foreign subsidiaries, a condensed statement of assets and liabilities, sales, income and dividends received could be provided by countries or regions. Many companies now present this type of information. Exhibit X shows how this information is disclosed by Eastman Kodak for its foreign subsidiaries.

(5) Information useful to analysts could be provided by a schedule supporting the investment account, showing the cost of each major investment, percent ownership interest, equity in net assets, dividends received and income earned by the subsidiary. Although it does not show all of this information, the American Smelting and Refining Company prepares such a schedule as shown in Exhibit XI on page 76.

(6) For significant unconsolidated subsidiaries engaged in distinctly different businesses such as finance or real estate companies, full or condensed balance sheets and income statements may be included in the annual report. This practice was found to be fairly common among the companies studied. In this connection, regulations relating to SEC Form S-1 contain the following provisions:

> "Subject to Rule 4-03 of Regulation S-X regarding group statements of unconsolidated subsidiaries, there shall be filed for each majority-owned subsidiary of the registrant not consolidated the balance sheets and profit and loss statements which would be required if the subsidiary were itself a registrant. Insofar as practicable, these balance sheets and profit and loss statements shall be as of the same date or for the same date or for the same periods as those of the registrant."

A few companies participating in this study also include in their annual reports condensed or full financial statements for certain major subsidiaries which are consolidated. This provides investors with financial information about segments which have a major impact on consolidated financial condition and earnings. A few companies participating in this study follow this practice (e.g., Kern

County Land Company, Martin Marietta, Southern Pacific, Transamerica).

(7) In preparing segment reports for product lines and markets, corporate entities are not significant and should be disregarded in order to show a complete picture of segment operations. However, in some instances a product line or market segment may also be a subsidiary for which separate segment reports are issued. Several companies participating in this study follow this practice.

EXHIBIT X

Financial Data for Foreign Subsidiaries

	Canada and Latin America	British Isles and Continental Europe	Africa, Asia, Australasia, and the Far East	TOTAL (After Interterritory Eliminations)	
	1966	1966	1966	1966	1965
			(in thousands)		
Net Assets					
Current assets	$ 50,517	$223,614	$34,562	$303,289	$261,811
Current liabilities	29,132	102,291	18,010	144,787	120,793
Working capital	$ 21,385	$121,323	$16,552	$158,502	$141,018
Properties and other assets	29,996	115,476	26,975	172,408	146,722
Total net assets	$ 51,381	$236,799	$43,527	$330,910	$287,740
Less: Interest of minority share owners	—	1,411	12	1,423	702
Equity of the Eastman Kodak Company	$ 51,381	$235,388	$43,515	$329,487	$287,038

Sales and Earnings

Sales	$109,596	$420,261	$63,728	$582,651	$495,661
Cost of goods sold	$ 71,380	$273,863	$42,939	$377,219	$319,902
Sales, advertising, distribution, and administrative expenses	16,174	65,222	10,585	91,981	77,567
Depreciation of properties and equipment	1,841	15,231	2,260	19,332	16,865
Total costs and expenses	$ 89,395	$354,316	$55,784	$488,532	$414,334
Earnings from operations	$ 20,201	$ 65,945	$ 7,944	$ 94,119	$ 81,327
Deduct: Other (income) and expense—net	$ 1,018	$ 3,270	$ 382	$ 4,670	$ 2,519
Provision for income taxes	10,017	26,960	3,364	40,341	35,794
	$ 11,035	$ 30,230	$ 3,746	$ 45,011	$ 38,313
Net earnings	$ 9,166	$ 35,715	$ 4,198	$ 49,108	$ 43,014

Eastman Kodak Company equity in:

Net earnings	$ 9,166	$ 35,402	$ 4,197	$ 48,793	$ 42,731
Dividends	3,095	11,933	1,691	16,719	14,058

The U.S. dollar equivalents in the above summary were computed generally at official exchange rates applied as follows:

1) net current assets at fiscal year-end rates,

2) property, plant, and equipment and the related reserves for depreciation at average rates prevailing during the year of acquisition of the assets, and

3) net earnings at average rates with the dollar equivalent adjusted for exchange differences resulting from the foregoing procedures.

From Eastman Kodak Company, 1966 Annual Report.

EXHIBIT XI

Supporting Schedule for Investment Account

INVESTMENTS

December 31, 1966	Shares Owned	Percent	Book Value (cost or less)	Market Value(a)
SUBSIDIARIES NOT CONSOLIDATED:				
Mount Isa Mines Limited	51,204,860	53.7	$12,603,022	$237,590,600
Southern Peru Copper Corporation	402,936	51.5	15,887,144	
Other			602,319	
			29,092,485	
COMPANIES OTHER THAN SUBSIDIARIES:				
Asarco Mexicana, S.A.	3,538,009	49.0	26,925,361(b)	164,246,000
General Cable Corporation (note 6)	4,848,590	36.1	4,223,173	4,953,100
Hecla Mining Company	117,930	4.8	3,578,920	9,948,900
Kennecott Copper Corporation	259,254	.8	2,541,657	46,555,600
Revere Copper and Brass Incorporated (note 6)	938,148	34.2	8,587,014	711,000
United Park City Mines Company	379,211	9.8	1,760,427	
Other			6,444,834	
			54,061,386	
TOTAL INVESTMENTS			$83,153,871	

(a) Amounts shown are based on December 31, 1966 quotations of stocks traded on the New York and London Stock Exchanges, but do not purport to represent the realizable or fair value of such large blocks of stock.

(b) Includes cost applicable to notes received in connection with sale of 51% interest to Mexican investors.

From American Smelting and Refining Company, 1966 Annual Report.

CHAPTER 6

Reactions of Corporate Executives to Segment Reporting

SUMMARY

If reactions of executives in the 70 companies included in this study are representative, there is no serious opposition to disclosure of segment sales. Opposition to disclosure of segment profits is generally strong, although there are exceptions. Major reasons advanced against disclosure reflect doubt that segment profit figures can be meaningful and usable to outsiders and fear that disclosure will bring detrimental reactions from competitors, customers, and others.

On the contrary, in the few companies which have actual experience with reporting of segment profit margins, executives interviewed expressed the opinion that disclosure had been beneficial because it had brought better understanding of the companies in the financial community. No objectionable results of consequence had been encountered by these companies.

Analysis suggests that carefully designed reporting techniques can meet major needs which investors and bankers have for information about segment profitability without serious damage to the reporting companies.

E~ACH EXECUTIVE INTERVIEWED~ in the 70 companies participating in the study was asked to express the attitude of his company's management toward inclusion of segment sales and profits in the company's annual report. Often two or more individuals were interviewed in the same firm. In terms of organizational responsibilities, these executives may be classified as follows: Presidents, Chairmen of Board, and Executive Vice Presidents (12); Vice Presidents of Finance (39); Controllers and Treasurers (35); Directors of Accounting and Assistant Controllers (23). In arranging interviews, opportunity to talk with company executives responsible for or familiar with external financial reporting policy was requested. Three of the 70 companies visited are excluded from the following discussion since they are essentially single industry firms.

GENERAL REACTIONS TO DISCLOSURE OF SEGMENT DATA

Segment Sales Reporting

From the summary of segment reporting practice given in Chapter 4 it seems apparent that vigorous opposition to reporting segment sales has virtually disappeared among companies participating in this study. Even those companies that presently are opposed to including this information in their annual reports do provide sales breakdowns in 10-K's filed with the SEC and many state that they furnish this information to analysts when requested.

Segment Profit Reporting

Based on the sample used in this study, corporate managements generally are strongly opposed to disclosing segment profits, although a slight trend away from this attitude is discernable. Nevertheless, most of these executives are convinced that disclosure in some manner shortly will be required. A summary of present practices and attitudes of the managements of the companies visited is shown below. Since the companies presently reporting segment profits were selected for this very reason, the sample is hardly typical of corporations generally.

	Number of Companies
Strongly opposed	36
Moderately opposed	16
Not opposed	4
Presently reporting segment profits ...	11
	67

The distinction between "strongly" and "moderately" opposed is, of course, judgmental and should not be overstressed. In the latter category, there at least was an awareness of the need for segment profits by investors and professional analysts and the opposition expressed tended to be somewhat muted. The following examples of statements by corporate executives whose companies are classified as moderately opposed to reporting segment profits may somewhat clarify this delineation.

"The trend in public reporting is toward disclosure of segment sales and profit margins. I would be restive but not completely negative to reporting margins for three major product categories."

"Although we regard ourselves as a progressive public-minded concern and probably will disclose more information in the future, we have certain reservations about showing income. We are great believers in disclosure if meaningful. But we are not convinced that breaking out a division which is losing money is meaningful and it could be misleading. Nevertheless, we are not vigorously opposed to this trend and probably will not resist it."

"I don't think we would be violently opposed to giving out more details."

"The investor has a right to know what is going on in the major segments of a business. However, we wouldn't be the first to disclose segment profits because this is a highly competitive industry. There would be no objection if competitors were required to make the same disclosure.

REASONS FOR OPPOSING REPORTING OF SEGMENT PROFITS

An awareness of the reasons for the opposition to disclosure of segment profits by so many corporate managements is fundamental to a resolution of the issue. In order to provide an indication of their relative importance, each adverse comment has been classified. Thus, in terms of frequency of occurrence, the reasons for opposition to reporting segment profits may be listed as shown at the top of the following page.

Belief That Data Will Not Be Meaningful

As indicated by the frequency of occurrence, a large number of corporate executives believe that information on segment profits will not be properly understood. They feel that the data will be misused even by competent analysts who are not familiar with the complexities of the company or the limitations of the data. These executives contend that segment profit reporting cannot be useful to investors or financial analysts in the absence of considerable ex-

	Reasons for Opposition to Reporting Segment Profits	*Frequency of* Occurrence
1.	Belief that data will not be meaningful	28
2.	Fear of competition	28
3.	The problem of revenue and cost allocations	21
4.	Organizational structure not amenable to segment profit reporting	12
5.	Segment classification difficulties	11
6.	Segments of different companies not comparable .	10
7.	Would interfere with proper discharge of managerial responsibilities	7
8.	Segment profits or losses not indicative of their contribution to company	5
9.	Concerned with long-term investor rather than short-term speculator	5
10.	Interests of stockholders and analysts differ	4
11.	Exposes management's pricing strategies	3
12.	Cost to prepare information	3
13.	Fear of prosecution by government agencies	3
14.	Will lead to demand for even more disclosure ...	2

planation relating to management strategies, product mix, nature of markets, product interrelationships, assumptions employed in preparation of data, long-term versus short-term considerations, etc. Some typical comments were as follows:

"The mix of diverse products and markets would preclude the usefulness of product data to analysts for forecasting. To report on all of these details would swamp the analyst with details."

"We would be reluctant to show losses for segments which have not as yet reached maturity. Stockholders might get wrong impressions."

"Analysts could not appraise the really important facts in profits, namely marketing development, management competence, manufacturing skills, research and development, etc. These are the things that make a company worth three times its book value."

"Outsiders might draw misleading conclusions because they wouldn't understand why management has taken certain actions or appreciate the fact that divisions and products often cannot be judged like independent businesses because they support each other."

"In defense industries segment profits would be misleading because we use percentage of completion to report long-term contract profits.

80

This is difficult to predict. There often are substantial subsequent major adjustments, not only because of bad estimates, but also because of penalties and incentives. Risk of prediction is great. We have a considerable mix of contracts. A breakdown of profits would not be meaningful."

"The usefulness of this information to the recipient is questionable. Many factors affect profits. It is not easy to even get managers to understand this, even though they know the business better than outsiders. There is a multiplicity of variables that limit even management's profit planning. I don't believe we would ever be able to supply information which would enable outsiders to make useful forecasts."

"Product P/L doesn't always measure economic importance to the company. Retention of individually unprofitable products may be desirable because these segments give access to profitable markets or to sources of profitable products."

"Divisions and products can't be judged like independent businesses because they support each other. That is why the company has expanded this way. Recently we entered a new business which is not very profitable, but we had to do it to protect the market and profits of an existing division."

The foregoing comments and others made in the course of interviews can be summarized in three principal points, namely: (1) that diversity and change in mix of products and markets preclude accurate impressions of the business or making of useful forecasts; (2) that analysts and investors cannot make forecasts of company earnings; (3) that investors will be confused or misled by segment data.

(1) While any summary of operations for a large diversified company obscures many details, the demand for segment reporting is an attempt to break down the single consolidated income statement into more significant pieces. Analysts feel that even a comparatively few broad segments are preferable to none. It seems likely that the manner in which activities are grouped into segments for reporting can help considerably to improve the usefulness of the information. As suggested earlier in this report, segments need to be as homogeneous as possible with respect to effects of outside economic influences and internal profit structure. Given such conditions, forecasts for groups of items may prove more accurate than forecasts for many individual items because some random factors may balance out. While another approach to the problem of mix diversity is to break out more segments for reporting, this action is limited, both by the number of separate forecasts the analyst can economically make and by the increased disclosure of information that may be used to the company's detriment by competitors and others.

(2) Some executives expressed opinion that analysts and investors lack technical competence to utilize relevant information for making forecasts. Others cited their own company's unsuccessful experience with forecasting with internal data at their command. While it must be granted that forecasting is subject to error, and that the margin of error is sometimes wide, it is impossible for investors to make rational decisions without making forecasts. With a return on his investment (dividends plus accretion in market value) as a goal, decisions to buy, hold, or sell are necessarily guided by expectations with respect to profits of those companies considered as investment alternatives. While many investors formerly made decisions more or less blindly because they lacked financial knowledge and very little reliable information was available, these conditions are no longer characteristic. The number and skill of professional analysts have increased rapidly in recent years. In addition, individual investors have become increasingly sophisticated. These assertions were supported by frequent comments from executives interviewed to the effect that forecasts by analysts are often close to those made by company personnel. In a few cases certain analysts' forecasts are valued as independent checks on management's outlook. Analysts' technical competence varies, as it does in other fields such as engineering, law, or management, but the most knowledgeable will likely continue to exert pressure for information which they believe they can use effectively.

(3) That investors will misunderstand or be misled is perhaps one of the oldest arguments that have been advanced against disclosure of company financial information. Nevertheless, interpreting reports for segments of a business requires understanding of the nature of segment operations and of the measuring techniques that can be used. Some education will be necessary and it seems possible that reporting companies can facilitate this process by explaining rather fully the accounting methods employed in preparing segment margin reports.

Fear of Competition

Much of the opposition to segment reporting by corporate executives is based on the presumption that this information will be used to a company's disadvantage by competitors and perhaps also by customers. It is feared that the disclosure of profits for a particular segment might lead competitors to shift their sales effort or bring new competitors into the industry. Customers might press for price reductions or decide to supply their own needs to save the supplier's profit. Concern was expressed about foreign competitors deriving benefit from reported segment profits, particularly since most foreign companies do not publish such data and are not subject to reporting requirements established in the U.S. Several executives were uneasy about revealing profitability of newer segments, especially when such activities were innovative, because competitors might reap benefits from research and development without contributing to the costs.

These and other arguments are reflected in such comments as:

"We have no objection to giving the stockholders anything they wish to know, but in their interest we have to consider reactions of competitors and governments, both domestic and foreign."

"Profit margins are extremely valuable proprietary information which competitors and unions could use to do great damage to the company's stockholders. This company prices on market strength, not on costs, and to reveal margins would destroy profit opportunities."

"The industry is a highly competitive one and we feel that disclosure would be a distinct disservice to the shareholders. It would be a way of forcing the aggressive and efficient company to give away useful information to its less efficient competitors."

"We would be concerned about revealing information to competitors. This is important in our industry because of bidding on government contracts."

"Another source of objection to product line profit reporting is that competitors—particularly foreign competitors—would react to the company's detriment. American chemical companies are engaged in worldwide competition; foreign competitors give no profit figures and can't be made to do so. This is a very important consideration to our company."

"We operate in 10 different industries. In some of these industries, we compete with family-controlled companies that don't have to report publicly. In these industries we perform a service which is fee-negotiated. We would be in an unfair position in negotiating contracts."

"When we started one of our major activities, it was innovative and we would not have wanted to reveal our profits because competitors might enter the field."

Where disclosure of segment sales and margins may bring reactions from competitors and customers that will do serious damage to a company's profits, the impact of this damage will fall on stockholders. Hence it may be expected that they would be willing to forego more information if they are aware of the facts. However, there seems to be evidence indicating that the situation is not one in which disclosure of segment operating results will be wholly good or bad in all cases.

In the first place, it may be questioned whether a significant amount of information valuable to competitors will be revealed in broadly based segment reports. It may be possible to disclose results for some segments but not for others, as suggested in one executive's comment:

> "This company now shows operating profit from its four divisions and dividends from partially-owned affiliated companies. Some of the latter issue their own financial reports. We would hesitate to reveal any breakdown by markets because competitors would quickly spot the profitable areas and move in when we are doing well in a certain market. We don't want to invite competitors by disclosure."

The superiority that a company enjoys over its competitors rests in conditions such as its managerial talent, technical competence, skill and loyalty of its employees, and financial resources. These are not likely to be visible in an income statement that covers a combination of products or markets. Owing to the fact that outsiders ordinarily will not know the the detailed content of nonseparable costs excluded in reporting contribution margins or how these costs are allocated when net margins are reported, absolute profitability of a segment will not be shown.

Companies are understandably reluctant to release individual product costs and margins, but this is not the kind of information asked for by financial analysts. Most of the executives interviewed readily admitted that they have substantially more information about competitors than proposed segment reports would provide, although reports sometimes might substantiate what are now only estimates of uncertain accuracy. Production processes are generally known and it was often stated that reasonably accurate approximations of competitor's costs and profits for specific items can be made. Among the companies that presently report segment profits, there was no mention of concern about competitive disadvantage resulting from disclosures made. A few executives commented to the effect that no company would have a net advantage if all were required to make similar disclosure.

While executives in 28 companies mentioned competition as a major factor underlying their opposition to disclosure of segment margins, executives in 15 companies (some in the same industries as opponents) stated that competition is a spurious argument. These attitudes are seen in comments below.

> "We aren't too much concerned about competition. All companies in our industry know each other's business pretty well."

> "Competition is not an important consideration provided individual product margins aren't disclosed."

"Competition is not a major problem. Our competitors can easily duplicate our products and figure out our profit margins."

"I don't believe competition can be raised as a valid excuse. Companies already know more about each other than would be disclosed in an income statement."

"Disclosure of information to competitors is no objection. In my opinion, too much stress is put on this factor. If competitors think they are fooling us by not reporting their profit margins, they are only fooling themselves."

There may, however, be individual circumstances in which disclosure would work hardship. For this reason any uniform rules which may be established to govern segment disclosure will need provision for exceptions where management can substantiate that material damage is likely to occur.

Looking at the broad picture, it seems likely that the availability of reliable information about company operations has been one factor in the expansion of markets for industrial capital in the United States. Management has often opposed increased disclosure, but in the long run the economy has benefitted from willingness of more individuals to invest in corporate securities. In countries where little information is available, relatively few individuals have been willing to invest in corporate securities.

Technical Problems

The technical problems encountered in developing segment reports have been discussed in Chapter 2. Many of the executives interviewed expressed serious concern over whether these problems can be satisfactorily solved. At the same time these comments showed that the problems take quite different forms in different companies. Provided an individual company is permitted to develop reporting patterns which are designed for its own organization structure and operating methods, many executives agreed that useful segment reports can be produced. On the other hand, all interviewees were doubtful that meaningful reports could be developed in conformance to any uniform classification of products.

Prevalence of joint costs and revenues was the source of technical problems most frequently mentioned. However, most executives feel that these problems are not insurmountable provided segments to be reported on can be chosen in such a way that jointness of costs and revenues is held to a minimum. Typical comments:

"A major problem is the allocation of expenses. Factory and direct marketing present no problems. Indirect marketing and central administration would have to be allocated largely on an arbitrary basis, although I suppose the allocation problem could be avoided by reporting gross margins."

"Product line reporting is used internally but management knows the basis of allocation. They also know how products relate to each other. If you deal with gross margins you omit a large chunk of management effort and capital used. However, this is not our major source of opposition. These problems can be licked although product line profits cannot be as precise as that for the entire company."

Characteristics of margins that might be developed without allocating joint revenues and costs were described in Chapter 2. It was also pointed out there that analysis indicates that useful margins can be ascertained only where operations have a substantial portion of separable costs and revenues. Even if reliable allocations could be made, investors would not have use for financial reports on segments of a highly integrated operation because it needs to be viewed as a single unit in making forecasts of income. Executives generally agreed with these conclusions.

Another technical problem of major concern to company executives is classification of segments for external reporting. There was general opposition to authoritative imposition of any uniform classification such as the Standard Industrial Classification on grounds that such classifications would be arbitrary and irrelevant to investors' purposes as well as burdensome to the reporting companies.

It is not a simple matter for a company to classify several thousands of products into a few broad groupings without losing significant facts. This is reflected in the following statements:

"Definition of a product group is an important decision for product line reporting. This company has 14 or 15 major product groups with perhaps 100 items in some groups. The same product is often sold to different users through different marketing channels."

"A classification of products would be necessary. I am concerned that a classification not natural to the business would be imposed on us for reporting purposes or that a classification once adopted might not be readily changed when the structure of the business changed. This would tend to destroy the significance of the figures."

"While it would be possible to report earnings for end products, this would defeat what management is trying to tell in its reports. A big expansion in electronics would not be seen because electronic items go into other products and would not be reported under the later category."

Most executives agreed that reasonably satisfactory classifications can be worked out if each company is permitted to develop a classification for its own operations. Exhibit XII shows the product classification used by the Eastman Kodak Company in its 1966 annual report.

EXHIBIT XII

Illustration of Listing of Items Included in
Product Line Categories

KODAK'S 1966 SALES DOLLAR: *$1,742 million*

41 PERCENT	28 PERCENT	22 PERCENT	9 PERCENT
APPLIED PHOTOGRAPHY	AMATEUR PHOTOGRAPHY	FIBERS, PLASTICS, AND INDUSTRIAL CHEMICALS	SPECIAL PRODUCTS
$720 MILLION	**$486 MILLION**	**$383 MILLION**	**$153 MILLION**
Photographic films, papers, plates, chemicals, equipment, and magnetic tape for: education and professional entertainment; medical, dental, and industrial radiography; micro-recording and information handling; office copying and duplicating; photofinishing; professional, commercial, and industrial photography; instrumentation and photofabrication; printing and publishing; mapping and aerial photography.	Photographic films for color prints, slides, and home movies (Kodacolor, Kodachrome, Ektachrome) and pictures in black-and-white (Verichrome Pan, Plus-X, Tri-X, Panatomic-X); cameras, projectors, lenses, and other photographic accessories; processing chemicals for home darkrooms; Kodak color print and processing services.	Polyester, modacrylic, and cellulosic fibers for apparel and home furnishings; cigarette filter material; polyethylene, polypropylene, polyallomer, and cellulosic plastics for packaging, wrapping, decorative sheeting, appliances, automotive parts, and many other applications; acids, adhesives, aldehydes, industrial alcohols, antioxidants, plasticizers, solvents, textile dyes, and other industrial chemicals.	Vitamin concentrates, monoglycerides, and organic chemicals for research; special military items; research and development under government contract; miscellaneous supplies and production equipment sold to Kodak manufacturing companies outside the United States.
In 1965: $600 million or 41 percent Percentage Change: +20 percent	In 1965: $404 million or 28 percent Percentage Change: +20 percent	In 1965: $334 million or 23 percent Percentage Change: +15 percent	In 1965: $125 million or 8 percent Percentage Change: +23 percent

1965 sales reclassified on a comparable basis

Executives frequently explained that many company accounting systems are not designed to produce periodic income statements by product classification. Examples of such comments are:

"We have no internal product line profit reports. Accounting is by management responsibilities which often cut across product lines. All transfer pricing is done at 'arms length.'"

"Each of our mills and converters buys and sells internally as well as externally. In a substantial part of our business, we don't know how materials will be used in terms of end products."

"The real problems of segment reporting are technical ones. Plastics are made by a company in which we have a 50% interest. These plastics are sold at market prices to our packaging division which sells to customers. Eliminating sales of the plastic division understates the true size of the corporation's operations."

"We would have to change our whole accounting system to eliminate interdivision profits. Our accounting system is designed to measure results by segments which are management centers of responsibility rather than by end products. Product costs are obtained by special studies when wanted for such purposes as pricing."

"The major difficulty is internal transfer pricing, although this would disappear if we grouped profits by end-products. But we don't do this internally."

"We have a considerable integration of divisions. For example, a corrugated box division supplies boxes for finished products and the interdivisional transfer price has a substantial effect on divisional profits. In order to have divisions organized as profit centers, transfers must be made at market price. The accounting system in use thus is designed to accumulate costs by managerial responsibilities rather than end products. It takes several months to work out product costs for internal planning purposes. While this is what the outsider wants, it is not practical to report in this way."

The problem is somewhat further complicated when certain of the segments are separate legal entities. Natural product groupings may not correspond with legal boundaries. Moreover, protection of minority interests requires that transfers between a parent and a less than 100% owned subsidiary be executed at bonafide prices. However, in the preparation of a consolidated income statement the parent company's share of unrealized profit must be eliminated. Complex though these problems may be, they are susceptible of solution—but at some cost to the companies.

Segment Data Not Considered Meaningful

An argument often advanced by executives against disclosure of segment results is that, in the absence of comprehensive knowledge of a company's operations, even the most competent analyst cannot use segment reports for making reliable forecasts of future income. To argue that outsiders cannot make forecasts of company income leads to the conclusion that rational selection of investments is impossible, although there are probably few who would defend this position. Moreover, in some companies where segment sales reporting was opposed as useless, segment sales and margins are disclosed to certain analysts either directly or indirectly by confirming analysts' estimates.

An argument which seems more plausible is based on the fear that recipients of segment statements will make unwarranted comparisons between what are mistakenly thought to be like segments in different companies. This concern and its implications are apparent in the following comments.

"Such figures wouldn't be comparable with other companies because of differences in product combinations and in accounting methods. Changing conditions within a company from period to period would also make such comparisons invalid. This might lead stockholders to draw erroneous conclusions and could even lead to stockholder suits."

"No matter what they say, analysts and others will make comparisons between product lines of different companies. Our paper products group includes six divisions with diverse characteristics. They are quite different from competitors."

"Analysts do not have sufficient understanding of the company's operations to make valid comparisons with competitors. For example, our gear division not only sells at wholesale and to industrial users but also to our own retail outlets. This would invalidate comparisons with competitors who market their products differently."

"Analysts always want to know which are the high and low cost producers and would inevitably compare our chemical division with other companies.

Evidence from interviews with financial analysts shows that the analysts who participated in the study understand very well the limitations of such intercompany comparisons. While some less knowledgeable analysts and investors may misuse segment information, they will tend to be eliminated by their own lack of success.

Statements which have a considerable degree of validity have been made to the effect that segment statements cannot reveal the interdependence of segments or measure what may be the major contributions an individual segment makes to the whole. Following are representative comments.

"Segment profits are not indicative of the total company effort. A conglomerate like this is more than the sum of its individual segments. Having many skills under a single corporate umbrella makes possible a total systems approach to serving markets and taking advantage of market opportunities. Often skills and people will be drawn from half a dozen divisions to develop a new idea and which division gets credit isn't important in the overall results. The financial reports for a conglomerate company need to stress the overall competence to serve markets economically. Profits recorded for individual segments are significant only for measuring segment management, not to the outsider whether creditor or stockholder."

"I, as a financial officer, don't care whether we are making or losing money in each sector in a given time period. I am concerned about the total, and so should our stockholders. For example, when we introduced ————, we spent a great deal on marketing and knew that we would lose money that year. It was a calculated loss and giving out this information might be misleading unless all the facts were known."

"It may be in the corporate interest to have the chemical division do research on a new material for plastic bottles when neither the chemical nor packaging division wished to do this work because they have short-range projects with priority. Thus, the short-term earnings of the divisions are sometimes subordinated to the long run interests of the whole corporation. This is the advantage of a conglomerate which isn't reflected in the operations of the individual segments."

"Product line statements do not show the harmony of the whole body. It is very important to have our products marketed through our stores even though the stores may not show very large profits. Management thinks in terms of the whole rather than individual segments."

Segment statements are short-run in nature and thus far no satisfactory method exists to measure the synergistic effect that is realized by having a segment in a combination rather than separated. Similar shortcomings attach to consolidated statements because these also are for short periods and fail to display long-run objectives and accomplishments for a company as a whole. Despite these limitations, it seems better to have partial measures rather than the alternative which is to rely on purely qualitative impressions. Knowledgeable users of financial statements seem unlikely to be misled.

Interference with Management's Function

Several executives expressed uneasiness about the potential influence which disclosure of segment results might have on management's decisions. Thus management might hesitate to take risks or to make investments with long period pay-offs if it was required to explain its actions to stockholders and possibly even defend itself against suits. Some comments of this type are given below.

"Analysts often obtain the impression that one company is less well managed than another where the difference is in the method of reporting or in the nature of the operations. This is a matter of concern to management because stockholders then ask questions which are difficult to answer satisfactorily. The same situation may also have an unfavorable effect on the market prices of some companies' stocks."

"Management would not feel free to make decisions in the long run interests of stockholders if it was subject to outside pressures based on short-run results."

"This would raise questions by stockholders as to why certain segment profits are low. For example, our government contract margins are low and we would be required to explain why we allocate costs that otherwise would be borne by other divisions to these contracts."

"We would be concerned about making investments that do not earn an adequate amount or are even losing money at the outset."

Several executives pointed out that management may be reluctant to report losses or low profits from some segments and that this might lead to an overly conservative attitude in decisions. Yet explanations of situations such as those described in the following excerpts from annual reports are not uncommon.

"Earnings of unconsolidated foreign subsidiary operations totalled $215,015 for the year. These earnings were adversely affected by the loss incurred by our Argentine subsidiary, as compared to a good profit in the prior year. This loss was caused principally by the rapid deterioration of the economy in that country. In line with Brazil's gradually improving economy, our Brazilian subsidiary, which incurred substantial losses in the past several years, showed considerable improvement and operated at slightly less than a break-even point." (Bausch & Lomb, 1966 Annual Report, p. 5)

"The performance of W. P. Fuller Paint Company, a wholly owned Hunt subsidiary, continued to be disappointing. Despite slightly improved sales, Fuller operated at a loss. Management is continuing its efforts to develop areas of profitability, reduce costs, and solve the problems of realigning Fuller's marketing and distribution programs. This revitalization will take more time, effort and money than had been expected . . ." (Hunt Foods and Industries, 1965 Annual Report, p. 18)

"The serious slump in housing brought on by tight money had a more pronounced impact on Company earnings. Sales of our gypsum and pipe products are largely dependent on housing starts. Flintkote is also a comparative newcomer in the gypsum and asbestos-cement pipe businesses, and has not yet had time to gain the distribution to maintain operations at a satisfactory cost level." (Flintkote, 1966 Annual Report, p. 3)

"While the gain in earnings was gratifying, it was not satisfactory in all respects. If it were not for losses incurred by our Sperry Gyroscope Division, our net income would have been substantially greater. As previously reported, we made adjustments at this division to absorb excess costs relating to the development and production of new products . . ." (Sperry Rand Corporation, 1966 Annual Report, p. 3.)

The question of unfavorable results for some segments had been faced by management in two of the companies now reporting segment profits. In one case, the chairman of the board stated that, in his opinion, frankness in disclosing such results improved the company's image in the financial community. In the other case an executive commented as follows:

"Senior management of this company has been willing to face the questions that are asked by outsiders. It feels that it ought to ask itself, why stay in a business if it isn't profitable? It is easier to deal with such questions in the beginning."

Keeping in mind that disclosure is proposed only for major segments, most analysts and investors probably feel that information and explanations in such cases are essential to investment decision-making. Moreover, analysts and others often detect such situations and management may find it better policy to deal with them forthrightly.

Objections to Providing Information for Speculators

A small group of executives expressed strongly the view that the proponents of segment reporting are primarily speculators toward whom these managers feel no obligation. This attitude is seen in the following comment by the Chairman of the Board in one company visited.

> "We believe the company's management should primarily be concerned with long-term rather than short-term stockholders. The latter are market-oriented and rely on security analysts. Their objective is to profit by short-run price changes. The long-term stockholder looks for security and earnings on investment over the long pull rather than for speculative gains. We deplore the increasing power of the institutional investor and the weight given to analysts' opinions. Product line profit statements do not further the long-term success of the company; rather, they are designed to advance the short-term interests of analysts."

Several executives distinguished the objectives of security analysts from those of their companies' stockholders in words such as these:

> "Analysts represent their own firms; the interests of shareholders and analysts differ. Analysts frequently use information for their own firm's investments first and then reveal it to outside clients. Management is responsible for informing stockholders, not analysts."

> "We are critical of security analysts, many of whom are stock touts. We are interested in our stockholders, not security analysts. The same professional restraints should be imposed on security analysts as on CPAs. They should be required to divulge sources of information, time spent on research, etc."

While some managements evidently prefer stockholders who retain their shares over long periods and select investments primarily on the basis of confidence in management rather than on short period financial performances, this is contrary to practices and trends among investors.

Individual investors have become more knowledgeable in the application of investment analysis methods although most probably also utilize the results of professional analysts' work in the form of security information services and advice offered by brokers. Institutional investors almost invariably employ professional analysts. In such an environment, investors are constantly searching for more attractive opportunities and shift their holdings quickly in response to changes in the outlook for company profits.[1] Securities prices respond to such changes. Under such conditions, the securi-

---

[1] There seems to be little information available as to how long stockholders retain their shares in a company. Turnover calculation for 1966 for the 70 companies participating in this study showed a range from 3% to 85%, with a mean of 10%. This is, of course, only a very rough indication of retention.

ties markets function best in directing the flow of capital when reliable information is available to guide investors' and speculators' decisions because successful companies will be the ones best able to obtain funds for expansion.

The substantial amount of time and effort devoted to relationships with analysts by high-level company executives seems sufficient evidence of the importance accorded this group by most managements.

REACTIONS FROM EXECUTIVES IN COMPANIES CURRENTLY REPORTING SEGMENT PROFITS

Attitudes of company executives generally opposed to segment profit reporting have been described and appraised in the preceding pages. To complete the picture, reactions from executives in companies now reporting segment profits are given below. Perhaps the most interesting feature of these comments is that they stress the benefits derived from such disclosures by these companies. There seems to be little concern over the dangers seen by opponents of segment profit reporting.

The number of companies currently reporting segment profits is relatively small. Exhibit XIII presents statements received in writing, with permission to quote, from executives of three companies. A comprehensive statement of the reasons why one company decided to report profits for product lines together with management's appraisal of the results achieved by this action was given in paper read by R. J. Brockman, Vice President—Finance, Wallace & Tiernan, Inc., at the NAA Annual Conference in June 1967. Relevant excerpts from this paper follow. For the sake of brevity, these excerpts are not in their original order.

"We pierced the corporate veils in our 1964 Annual Report when we published for the first time a breakdown of the operating results of our three product line groups—chemicals, industrial equipment, and pharmaceuticals—on a separate page in the report immediately following the President's letter. . . . We did it not as a pioneering adventure or by compulsion to establish a precedent for others but solely because it met our particular needs and offered interesting opportunities and benefits to us.

"In 1964, the year we commenced reporting by product line, the distribution of sales among the three groups was chemicals 39%, equipment 32%, and, pharmaceuticals 29%.

"It was not much different in 1966. On the other hand, the swing

93

EXHIBIT XIII

Statements from Executives of Companies Reporting
Segment Profits

We believe that our decision is a pioneering step in providing stockholders and members of the financial community with information which we feel will be of significant help to them in appraising the current investment values inherent in the Company and its prospects for the future.

National Distillers and Chemical Corporation is perhaps unique in its areas of operation. We are major factors in liquors, chemicals and plastics, and copper and brass mill products, and we have growing interests abroad. In most instances, security analysts are industry specialists concerned primarily with one or another of the industries in which we participate. It is extremely difficult for them to appraise the Company as a whole without specific financial information about each of the industries in which we do business. We are convinced that by supplying such information we are making it possible for them to come to a more balanced judgment about our Company than they previously could.

As to possible competitive injury, we take the position that if each of our operating divisions were independent companies—as all except our International Division once were—they would be required to make full disclosure of their operating results and still meet the competition. Further, this information is available to any stockholder who may ask for it. We feel that, for our Company, the gains far outweigh any possible disadvantages that full disclosure implies. In arriving at divisional operating profits, divisions have been charged only with those operating expenses directly incurred by such divisions. On the income statement for 1966 you will note an item of $6,424,000 for "corporate and general expenses." This amount includes those expenses which are not directly associated with any single division and would have to be allocated to divisions on some arbitrary basis. Until such time as there is general acceptance of a formula for allocating such expenses, we propose to continue reporting same in a lump sum.

In addition, we have 50 per cent interests in four domestic affiliated companies in which other corporations share equal ownership. We take our share of their net profits (or losses) after taxes into our income statement by the equity accounting method and this figure is reflected in the operating profit of our Chemical Division. One of these companies, Reactive Metals, Inc., is one of two integrated producers and fabricators of titanium in the country. While we have no current intention of using other than a net figure for these affiliated companies, we believe that this is an important indication of the progress being made in areas where significant future growth is possible.

W. P. MARSH, Jr., *President*
National Distillers and Chemical Corporation

We feel that the use of this type of statement is appropriate to the multi-divisional company such as ours. Sharcowners and security analysts may tend to ignore the investment potential of such companies if unaware of the proportion of earnings derived from each industry in which the company operates.

94

EXHIBIT XIII (Continued)

In our case, the statement itself was a natural extension of our internal reporting. Since no allocation of corporate administration or interest on general corporate debt is made, the technical problems surrounding the allocation of these items are absent. While our competitors are now aware of our earnings from each division, we feel they had probably developed the information themselves before we made the presentation.

Although there have been problems, we have received favorable comment on our treatment, and hope that it has fulfilled its goal of bringing more information to our share owners, present and future.

DWIGHT M. COCHRAN, *President*
Kern County Land Company

Glidden management firmly believes that the Annual Report is one of the best opportunities available to frankly and completely inform our shareholders of our objectives and accomplishments and our problems. To understand a company of our size and diversity, we believe it essential to furnish information indicating the relative importance and trend of sales and profits in each of the major operating areas, which are Durkee Foods, Coatings and Resins, and Specialty Chemicals. We are often asked if the disclosure of this information results in a competitive disadvantage. I do not believe it does. The advantage we gain in better understanding is, in my opinion, a much more important consideration.

WILLIAM G. PHILLIPS, *President*
The Glidden Company

---

in the earnings contribution by the three groups between 1964 and 1966 was quite marked.

	1964	1966
Chemicals	45%	45%
Equipment	17%	27%
Pharmaceuticals	38%	28%

"As you can well appreciate, profit margins between the groups vary significantly and the percentage contribution to earnings is not necessarily the same as the percentage contributions to sales.

"We know the company was not well known. When there was recognition, more frequently than not it was with the original product line of chlorinators. In short, we had a problem which in the final analysis appeared to be largely one of inadequate communications. Our conventional method of reporting appeared to fall short of conveying the full Wallace & Tiernan story and the basic characteristics of the business.

"What is management's responsibility to its owners and others? What information do those who have a sincere interest in the business want? The answers at which we arrived clearly indicated that reporting on the classical basis fell short of meeting the valid needs of stockholders and others.

"In assessing the completeness of the information contained in our traditional reports we found we were not providing much of the basic data that was being sought. In the absence of a policy decision to release product line information, management was in the frustrating and awkward position of attempting to develop sound relationships of respect and confidence with its stockholders and others and yet constrained from a meaningful, frank discussion of our several businesses. Often an interview took on many of the aspects of a parlor game. As would be expected under such circumstances, a vacuum develops between the members of the financial community and the company for which we in the management had to take most of the responsibility. Not only did this inhibit the development of a relationship of mutual respect but in the absence of factual data, many analysts, being human, made bad guesses concerning the sources of the company's earnings and its future outlook. All too often this resulted in misinformation being circulated about the company which we were not well equipped to refute. . . .

"There are probably those who might ask why we did not choose to release certain data about the company to a privileged few—maybe just to those who thought to ask for it. This, however, would violate a principle that most people consider fundamental which precludes granting any information of importance that is not promulgated to all on an equal basis.

"Since the financial community has a propensity to assign different price/earnings ratios to the different operations of a diversified company, it appeared helpful, in order to have the company evaluated fairly, to disclose the relative earnings contribution of each of the major product groups. In our case, a breakdown of sales alone could be misleading due to the wide disparity in profit margins.

"Segmented reporting could also help focus attention on the inherent strengths and advantages that come from marketing a diverse line of products to different consuming industries serving different parts of the economy. Such information could be helpful to stockholders and others in assessing the impact on the company of changes in the economic or political sphere. Having definitive information of this type to discuss is also particularly useful to the management of a multifaceted company since, more often than not, you are faced with stockholders or analysts whose experience covers a limited number of industries and generally not all of those in which you are operating. Their education comes much easier with segmented details to discuss. This is important because those following your company should thoroughly understand and appreciate the fundamentals of the business, its products, its markets and its management—only then can they make a fair assessment of its present condition and future potential.

"We knew this might possibly give aid and comfort to the competition but in the final analysis we had to admit that usually competitors are fairly well informed about each other's operations, generally from trade sources, vendors, salesmen, contractors, ex-employees, and the like, so that they did not have to rely for their prime source of commercial intelligence on public disclosure in a stockholder's report. If you have ever done any market research or investigated an industry you know that competitors usually know what is going on. Then too, quite frankly, we knew we should not be revealing individual product line data but group data of a composite nature . . . We concluded that the adverse competitive threat was not a truly valid argument, in our case, for not reporting.

"For us at Wallace & Tiernan, line of business reporting has served the company's interests well and apparently the public's interest also. It has helped us display the strengths of our diversified company through better understanding. The gains have far outweighed any possible disadvantage."

Examination of annual reports to stockholders from companies disclosing segment profit margins seems to show that meangingful information about segment operations can be given. Executives in these companies generally expressed the opinion that such disclosure has been beneficial while no serious unfavorable reactions have occurred. Experience of these companies seems to suggest that segment reports must be carefully designed to present the individual company's operations in a useful way while avoiding potential dangers from disclosing sensitive information.

CHAPTER 7

Conclusions

1. *Evidence obtained in this study shows that investors and creditors have an important need for operating results of major segments of diversified companies.* The study utilized depth interviews with 72 financial analysts and 71 commercial bankers to ascertain how skilled users of financial reports employ information derived from these reports for making investment and credit decisions. Interviewees were virtually unanimous in the opinion that valid evaluations of investment and credit worth require knowledge of the magnitude of a diversified company's participation in each industry and the contribution made to consolidated profits.

2. *Disclosure of sales and contributions to consolidated profits is needed for segments which are affected differently by economic conditions, which have differing rates of profitability, and which make material contributions to company sales and earnings.* A primary function of the analyst is to forecast earnings. In working with diversified companies, these forecasts are first made for major industries and markets. Utilizing data drawn from company financial reports, income projections are made giving effect to expected economic conditions for each segment and then combined for conversion to earnings per share for the company being studied. This is, in effect, a simulation of the same internal procedures many companies use in forecasting and budgeting.

3. *No standard classification of segments for reporting can yield meaningful results when applied to companies with diverse organi-*

99

zational patterns. Moreover, uniformity for all companies is not essential because skilled analysts do not regard intercompany comparisons of segment results to be significant in their work. From the investor's standpoint, segments need to be homogeneous in the sense that their components are affected in the same way by economic conditions which influence earnings. In most cases, broad groups of end products constitute the significant segments. The nature of each group can be described by listing or describing products included, with explanation and adjustment of comparative statements when changes in classification are made. In some circumstances markets are also significant segments to outsiders when differences such as those between domestic and foreign or civilian and military markets have an important bearing on risks and profits. The types of segment earnings data desired by government agencies concerned with anti-trust and fair trade practices differ from the types of data needed by investors.

4. *Management in each company can best define the segments for which to report provided information needs expressed by investors and creditors are met.* Classifications relevant to outsiders will, in some cases, cut across divisional responsibility reporting segments employed in a company's internal financial reporting.

5. *Segment contribution margins constitute the most reliable and useful measures of segment profitability where there are material amounts of joint revenue and cost.* Disclosure of sufficient detail to enable users of segment reports to distinguish short-run variable, annual programmed, and long-run capacity costs will be helpful in forecasting earnings. Some of this information is now obtained by analysts through questioning of company executives.

6. *No serious opposition to disclosures of segment sales was found.* Disclosures of segment sales are often omitted from annual financial reports, but included in reports filed with the SEC. Stockholders' access to this information would be improved by inclusion in annual reports.

7. *With some exceptions, opposition to disclosure of segment contributions to profits is strong among company executives interviewed in the study.* Two major reasons for opposing disclosure of segment earnings were given by company executives.

a. Those opposed often expressed opinion that earnings figures meaningful to outsiders cannot be constructed for anything less than the whole enterprise. Evidence collected in the study indicates that some company executives underrate analysts' sophistication and skill in using financial reports. More important, this objection emphasizes the need to develop new reporting techniques such as the contribution margin approach described in this study.

b. Opponents also expressed fear that disclosure of segment earnings figures may provoke reactions from outsiders detrimental to interests of shareholders. Such danger is minimized by the fact that outsiders' information needs can be met with comparatively broad segments and without disclosing data for individual products. Segment reporting practices need to be sufficiently flexible to avoid disclosure which would be harmful to a company's shareholders and creditors.

8. *Executives of those companies which now report segment earnings stated that the practice has brought better understanding of their companies in the financial community with no objectionable reactions of consequence.*

9. *The investor's confidence in reports on segment operations will be improved if covered by the auditors' opinion.* In the United Kingdom where segment reporting is now required by the Companies Act, three major organizations of accountants have recommended that independent auditors should take responsibility for segment reports presented by management. This recommendation was stated as follows in a joint memorandum to the Board of Trade from the Institute of Chartered Accountants in England and Wales, Institute of Chartered Accountants of Scotland, and Association of Certified Corporate Accountants:[1]

> "Clause 17—Directors' report to state, where business of certain different classes carried on, attribution of turnover to, and profitability (or otherwise) of, business of each class.
>
> "66. The accountancy bodies consider that the analysis required by Clause 17 should be made a statement 'annexed' to the accounts and thus removed from the directors' report. The requirement will confront many companies with difficult problems of interpretation, allocation and presentation to which the answers will be matters of opinion involving, perhaps extensively, the exercise of judgment. This, however, is a feature of many problems which already arise in drawing up accounts. Moreover the information called for is accounting information which may itself be highly relevant to the presentation of a true and fair view of the results of the year. For these reasons it seems proper that the opinion of the directors as expressed in the information which is given should be subjected to the judgment of the auditors."

While management has primary responsibility for external reports, investors in the United States can be expected to place more credence in segment operating results if auditors accept responsibility for the data. This will require independent certified public

---

[1] *The Accountant,* January 28, 1967, p. 111.

accountants to satisfy themselves that segments reported on give a meaningful picture of a company's operations and that segment contributions to consolidated earnings are useful for purposes for which investors can be expected to use the information. This research study provides initial guidance for resolving these problems.

Development by each company of methods for reporting pertinent information about operations of its segments promises to be the best way to meet investors' and creditors' needs with a minimum of cost to reporting companies. If management fails to take the initiative in providing such information, rigid and detailed reporting requirements may be imposed on management. This course is likely to produce information of uncertain quality and to force companies to disclose sensitive data not essential to investor's purposes.

SELECTED BIBLIOGRAPHY

Barr, Andrew, "Comments on the Conglomerate Reporting Problem," *Financial Executive*, November 1967.

Barr, Andrew, "Need for Product Line Reporting," *Journal of Accountancy*, January 1968.

Bows, Albert J., Jr., "Problems in Disclosure of Segments of Conglomerate Companies," *Journal of Accountancy*, December 1966.

"Disclosure of Supplemental Financial Information by Diversified Companies," Statements in Quotes, *Journal of Accountancy*, October 1967.

"Divisional Profit Reporting by Public Corporations," *Forbes*, July 15, 1966.

Goodrich, Keith, "Executives' View of Corporate Reporting Responsibilities," *Financial Executive*, December 1966.

Holsen, Robert C., "The Problem of Conglomerates," *Ernst & Ernst Symposium for Educators*, Ernst & Ernst, 1967.

Lanterman, Joseph B., "How to Resolve the Financial Reporting Controversy," *Financial Executive*, December 1966.

Mautz, Robert K., "Bases for More Detailed Reporting by Diversified Companies," *Financial Executive*, November 1967.

Mautz, Robert K., "Conglomerate Reporting and Data Reliability," *Financial Executive*, September 1967.

Mautz, Robert K., "Financial Reporting by Conglomerate Companies," *Financial Executive*, February 1968.

Mautz, Robert K., "Identification of the Conglomerate Company," *Financial Executive*, July 1967.

"New Disclosures Noted in Annual Reports," *Financial Executive*, June 1967.

Rappaport, Louis H., "Problems in Product Line Reporting," *Lybrand Journal*, Vol. 48, No. 142, 1967.

Schachner, Leopold, "Corporate Diversification and Financial Reporting," *Journal of Accountancy*, April 1967.

Sommer, A. A., Jr., "Conglomerate Disclosure: Friend or Foe," *Journal of Accountancy*, May 1967.

Top Management Looks at Product-Line Reporting, Machinery & Allied Products Institute and Council for Technological Advancement, Washington, D.C., May 1967.

Wassner, Neil A., "Business Organization in the 21st Century—the Conglomerate," *Viewpoint*, Spring 1967.

COOPERATING CORPORATIONS

A C F Industries, Inc.
Air Reduction Co., Inc.
Allied Chemical Corp.
Aluminum Co. of America
American Can Co.
American Cyanamid Co.
American Home Products Corp.
American Machine and Foundry Co.
American Radiator & Standard Sanitary Corp.
American Smelting & Refining Co.
American Zinc, Lead & Smelting Co.

Bausch & Lomb, Inc.
Beckman Instruments, Inc.
Blaw-Knox Co.
Bristol-Myers Co.

Carnation Co.
Celanese Corp. of America
Colt Industries, Inc.
Continental Can Co.
Continental Oil Co.
Corn Products Co.
Crowell-Collier & Macmillan, Inc.
Crown Zellerbach Corp.

Eastman Kodak Co.
Emerson Electric Co.

Fibreboard Paper Products Corp.
The Flintkote Co.
FMC Corp.

General Dynamics Corp.
General Electric Co.
General Foods Corp.
The Gillette Co.

Hooker Chemical Corp.
Hunt Foods & Industries, Inc.

International Business Machines Corp.
International Paper Co.

International Telephone & Telegraph Co.

Jones & Laughlin Steel Corp.

Kaiser Aluminum & Chemical Corp.
Kaiser Industries Corp.
Kern County Land Co.

Litton Industries, Inc.

Martin Marietta Corp.
McDonnell Aircraft Corp.
McGraw-Hill, Inc.
McKesson & Robbins, Inc.
Monsanto Co.

National Distillers & Chemical Corp.

Ogden Corp.
Olin Mathieson Chemical Corp.

Philip Morris, Inc.
Pittsburgh Plate Glass Co.

Ralston Purina Co.
Raytheon Co.
Rexall Drug & Chemical Co.
Rockwell-Standard Co.

SCM Corp.
The Singer Co.
Southern Pacific Co.
Sperry Rand Corp.
Standard Oil Co. of California

Textron, Inc.
Transamerica Corp.
Union Carbide Corp.
Uniroyal, Inc.
United Merchants & Manufacturers

Varian Associates

Wallace & Tiernan, Inc.
Westinghouse Electric Corp.

Xerox Corp.

COOPERATING BANKS

Bank of America National Trust & Savings Association, *San Francisco, California*
Bank of Delaware, *Wilmington, Delaware*
Bank of New York, *New York, New York*
Bankers Trust Co., *New York, New York*
Brown Brothers Harriman & Co., *New York, New York*

Central Penn National Bank, *Philadelphia, Pennsylvania*
Chase Manhattan Bank, *New York, New York*
Chemical Bank New York Trust Co., *New York, New York*
City National Bank & Trust Co., *Kansas City, Missouri*
Commerce Trust Co., *Kansas City, Missouri*
County Trust Co., *White Plains, New York*
Crocker-Citizens National Bank, *San Francisco, California*

Fall River National Bank, *Fall River, Massachusetts*
First National Bank of Allentown, *Allentown, Pennsylvania*
First National Bank of Boston, *Boston, Massachusetts*
First National Bank, *Kansas City, Missouri*
First National Bank of Topeka, *Topeka, Kansas*
First National City Bank, *New York, New York*
First Pennsylvania Bank and Trust Co., *Philadelphia, Pennsylvania*
Franklin National Bank, Mineola, New York

Hartford National Bank, *Hartford, Connecticut*

Irving Trust Co., *New York, New York*

Manufacturers Hanover Trust Co., *New York, New York*
Marine Midland Grace Trust Company of New York, *New York, New York*
Morgan Guaranty Trust Co. of New York, *New York, New York*

National Shawmut Bank of Boston, *Boston, Massachusetts*

Philadelphia National Bank, *Philadelphia, Pennsylvania*
Provident National Bank, *Philadelphia, Pennsylvania*

Security First National Bank, *Los Angeles, California*
Society National Bank of Cleveland, *Cleveland, Ohio*
State Street Bank & Trust Co., *Boston, Massachusetts*

United California Bank, *Los Angeles, California*

Wells Fargo Bank, *San Francisco, California*

COOPERATING BROKERAGE AND INSTITUTIONAL INVESTMENT FIRMS

Abraham & Co.

Bache & Co., Inc.
The Bank of New York
Bear, Stearns & Co.
Blair & Co., Inc.
Boston Fund, Inc.
Brown Brothers Harriman & Co.

Clark, Dodge & Co., Inc.
Cyrus J. Lawrence & Sons

Dean Witter & Co.
Dominick & Dominick, Inc.
Donaldson, Lufkin & Jenrette, Inc.
Drexel Harriman Ripley, Inc.

Faulkner, Dawkins & Sullivan

Goldman, Sachs & Co.
Goodbody & Co.

Harris, Upham & Co.
Hayden, Stone, Inc.
H. Hentz & Co.
Hirsch & Co.
Hornblower & Weeks-Hemphill,
    Noyes

E. F. Hutton & Co. Inc.

Kuhn, Loeb & Co.

Lehman Brothers
Loeb, Rhoades & Co.

Massachusetts Investors Trust, Inc.
Merrill Lynch, Pierce, Fenner & Smith
    Inc.
Model, Roland & Co., Inc.

Newburger, Loeb & Co.

R. W. Pressprich & Co.
Putnam Mutual Funds, Inc.

Scudder Stevens & Clark, Inc.
Shields & Company
Standard & Poor's Corp.
State Street Investment Fund
Stroud & Co.

United States Trust Co.

Wainright & Co.
G. H. Walker & Co.
Walston & Co., Inc.
White, Weld & Co.
Wood, Struthers & Winthrop